What Happend to People?
Shizuoka Air Raid Documentary
-Real Voices from Japanese Small City-

Cover Illustration by Noriko Mizuno
Pages designed by Tomohiro Sugiyama

What Happened to People?
Shizuoka Air Raid Documentary
−Real Voices from Japanese Small City−

Hiroko Niitsuma
ISBN978-4-7838-2230-1 C0031

Published by Shizuoka Shimbun Co.,
3-1-1 Toro, Suruga-ku, Shizuoka 422-8033 Japan
Tel. +81-544-284-1666

All rights reserved.

© Shizuoka Shimbun Co., Shizuoka 2010

Printed in Japan

English | Japanese
対 訳

What Happend to People?
Shizuoka Air Raid Documentary
-Real Voices from Japanese Small City-

空から戦争がふってきた
静岡・空襲の記録

Hiroko Niitsuma

新妻 博子 著

静岡新聞社

Preface

My hometown, Shizuoka is the local city located about 180 km southwest of Tokyo. The first *Shogun* of the Tokugawa lived in the Sunpu Castle after he had his son take over *Shogunate* in the Edo era.

My family moved to Shizuoka city in 1978, where we could see Mt. Fuji. I did not know that there were air raids in Shizuoka city on June 20, 1945 until I spoke with air raid survivors at that time when my daughters were in elementary school about 20 years ago. I had known air raids from several books on Nagasaki, Hiroshima and Viet Nam, hearing the survivor's stories was a different experience from reading books.

I realized that it is necessary to let many people know – not only people in Japan but also people of other nations – the realities of the air raids. Shizuoka air raids were conducted with the conventional weapons. People could imagine the horror of air raids using conventional weapons much more than the use of nuclear weapons, for this purpose I started research on Shizuoka air raids with a hope to prevent future wars. Many people including children and women were bombarded and killed almost on a daily basis in the Gulf War. It was the same with the Japanese who had suffered from the air raids in World War II. Once a war starts, it would never stop utill one side is completely in ruins. Nations fight wars, but it is the individuals who are wounded and killed by wars. It was frustrating because I could do nothing to stop the ugly reality.

After 20 years since then, my dream finally came true with this book.

I fortunately met a young scholar – Mr. Cary Karacas from New York, in summer 2009. His sympathy and warm encouragement solved my concerns on how American people would find the contents. My friend, Chisako who had the aim focus to publish this book under medical treatment, passed away just on the same day I met Mr. Karacas. These two events gave me courage to head for publication.

まえがき

静岡は，東京の約180ｋｍ南西にある一地方都市です．江戸時代には，徳川家の初代将軍が隠居した後，駿府城に住んでいました．

私の家族が，静岡市へ転居してきたのは1978年，ここからはいつでも富士山が見えました．でも，静岡市が1945年6月20日に空襲を受けたことを知ったのは，子どもが小学生の頃，ずいぶん遅い目覚めでした．広島・長崎，ベトナム戦争での爆撃を本で何となく知っているつもりでいました．でも，体験者のお話が，私の思い上がりを打ち砕きました．

「あの空襲の実態を日本の人々だけではなく，外国の人々に伝えたい．空襲は，現在も使われている通常兵器によるもの，それだけに想像をはるかに超える核兵器よりも，現実的に世界に訴えることができるかもしれない」．このだいそれた考えが，本気で静岡空襲を調査するきっかけとなり，私を突き動かしてきました．その頃，湾岸戦争で毎日のように，子どもや女性を含む大勢の人々の命が奪われ，イラクの人々と当時の日本人が重なって見えました．いったん始まった戦争は，一方を叩きのめすまで止まらず，国家が起こした戦争の結末を一身に負うのは，個人なのです．こんな時，何もできない自分をもどかしく思っていた時期でした．

それから約20年，やっと念願の静岡空襲の英語版ができました．

この内容が果たしてアメリカ人の心に届くのだろうか，と少し不安に思っていた時，幸運にもニューヨークの若い研究者Cary Karacasさんに出会いました．2009年の夏のことです．彼の共感と温かい励ましが，出版を大きく後押ししてくれました．そしてちょうどその日，この本の出版を共に目指してきた闘病中の友人，桜井知佐子さんが旅立ちました．この2つの出来事が，前に進む勇気を与えてくれました．

In the past 20 years, documents of World War II are disclosed to public of which three sources of information are available at present: the stories of those who experienced the air raids; the historical documents in Japan; and public archives in the United States. We are now able to specify the mission of each air raid and why Shizuoka city was attacked.

It takes long time that the mission of on-going war to be revealed. I would like to present the compact model of Shizuoka air raids in 1945 — how it started, how it was carried out, what happened to people, how many people were killed, and how they died — as a means to prevent wars. Unlike during World War II, we can obtain daily food now in Japan. We no longer need to fear shells flying overhead. We can investigate the archives in Japan and the United States, and make our findings open to the public. Only a few people in the world have this kind of opportunity.

This book lines up English and Japanese side by side because I would like young Japanese readers in addition to English readers to read this book. I wish that those who do not know "air raids" like the way I used to be, would read this book. I made the whole text short with many photographs, paintings and exhibits so that readers can finish reading the serious theme at one time. I also included information from the U.S. military documents in it to show why and how Shizuoka city was attacked. Please remember that Shizuoka is just one of the many cities suffered from air raids and that there are many other cities in the world which did or are still suffering air raids.

I hope that this book would be in memories of many people.

　一方，この20年間で第2次世界大戦の記録は公開され，私たちは，空襲体験者のお話，日本側の記録，およびアメリカの公文書，の3つの視点から空襲をより包括的に理解できるようになりました．それぞれの空襲の作戦意図が特定でき，なぜ静岡市が空襲されたのかを知ることができます．

　現在進行中の戦争で，その作戦意図が明らかになるのは，ずっと後のこと．ならば1945年，私たちの街で起こった空襲の実態 — どういう流れの中で起き，どのように実行され，その結果人々はどのような状況におかれ，どれだけの人々がどのように亡くなったのか — をまるごとコンパクトに正確な事例として，外国の人々にも提供できれば，戦争を防ぐための一助となるのではないか，と思うのです．今私たちは，毎日の糧を得ることができ，頭上を飛び交う弾丸に恐れる必要もなく，自由に内外の公文書を調べ，発信できます．このような立場の人間は，実は世界でも数少ないかも知れません．

　この本は英語と日本語を併記しています．英語を話す人々はもちろん，日本の人々にも読んでいただきたいという思いからです．空襲を知らない人に，手にとっていただけたらうれしいです．内容は重いのですが，ページを開く手が重くならないように，一気に読める程度にページ数を抑え，多くの写真や絵や図を資料として配しました．特に，米国立公文書館所蔵の米軍資料を収録しました．なぜ，どのようにして，私たちの街が焼かれたのかを知ることができます．静岡は，過去から現在に至るまで，爆撃にさらされた数多くの街の「一つ」なのです．

　この本が，国境を越えて，多くの人々の目に留まりますように．

Remarks

1) This book has been designed as a thorough reference both in Japanese and English. However, we believe that it is not necessary to provide every detailed matching between two languages. Since it is almost impossible to translate the original Japanese place names into English, we are sure that it is preferable to spell those names in Roman letters or sometimes particular names are shown only in English.

2) You may recognize the different sizes and the forms of the translation within the captions for the charts and the photos in this book. Due to the requirement for the clear recognition for the readers, we dare to employ various forms. If the explanation is too long, we put the Japanese translation lines into box of broken lines. Also, the Japanese translations within diagram, we put them into the shading rectangles.

3) In this book, American "short" ton is used as a unit of weight instead of metric ton.
   We use the other units in this book as follows.
   - 1 ton (short ton) = 2,000 pounds = 907 kg
   - 1 pound (ld) = 453.6 g
   - 1 acre = 0.4047 ha (hectare) = 4047 m^2
   - 1 feet = 30.48 cm
   - 1 mile = 1.609 km
   - 1 gallon (U.S. gallon) = 3.78 l

4) In this book, Shizuoka city, Shimizu city and Kambara town represented the old ones respectively. Present Shizuoka city has combined neighboring Shimizu city, Kambara town, Yui town, since 2003.

凡例

1) 本書は英語でも日本語でも利用できるように構成されているが，国名や地名については，一部英語表記のみ，日本の地名についてはローマ字表記だけにするなど，必ずしも逐語的翻訳を試みてはいない．

2) 収録した図表，写真は，できる限り大きく見せるため，各説明（キャプション）のフォントサイズや和訳の位置が異なる．また，その説明が長い場合は，和訳を破線の囲みにし，図中の和訳は網掛けとした．

3) 本書では重量の単位として，メートル法のトンではなくアメリカで使用わされているショートトン（米トン）を使用．そのほか，本書で使用している単位は以下を参照．
   - 1トン（米トン）=2000ポンド=907キログラム
   - 1ポンド=453.6グラム
   - 1エーカー=0.4047ヘクタール=4047平方メートル
   - 1フィート=30.48センチメートル
   - 1マイル=1.609キロメートル
   - 1ガロン（米ガロン）=3.78リットル

4) 本書の「静岡市」，「清水市」，「蒲原町」は，旧市・町を指す．現在の静岡市は，2003年以来，近隣の清水市，蒲原町，由比町と合併してできた．

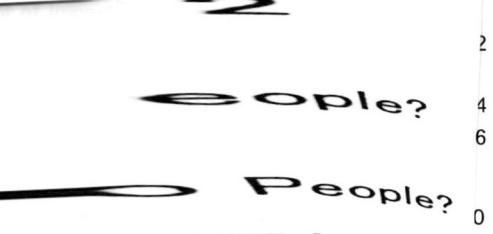

2. 3期に区分される空襲	26	
3. 転換点となった東京大空襲	27	
4. 静岡地域への空襲の概略	31	
5. 市街地空襲前夜:		
4月4日 三菱工場への爆撃	34	

Ⅳ. 静岡はなぜ, どのように空襲されたのか
1. なぜ静岡は空襲されたのか　36
2. 静岡空襲の準備と実行　38
   - 航空目標フォルダー　39
   - 地域コード付地図　41
   - リト・モザイク　42
   - 偵察写真（空襲前）　43
   - 目標情報票　43
   - 野戦命令書　44
   - 偵察写真（空襲後）　45
   - 損害評価報告書　46
   - 任務要約　47
   - 作戦任務報告書　48

Ⅴ. 絵と写真が語る静岡の空襲
1. 6月20日　静岡空襲　50
   - (1) 2時間で燃え尽きた街　50
   - (2) 炎の嵐の中を　52
   - (3) 安倍川へ　55
   - (4) 一夜明けて「私,生きていた…」57
2. 7月7日　清水空襲　61
3. 7月31日　艦砲射撃　63
4. 8月1-2日　最後の清水空襲　64
5. 空襲は続く…　65
6. 廃墟の街から　66
7. 慰霊　68

謝辞　70
参考文献　71

---

1. The beginning of air raid over Japanese mainland	24
2. Three stages of Air Raid	26
3. Tokyo Air Raid was the turning point	27
4. Outline of the air raid on the Shizuoka area	31
5. Before urban Air Raid: April 4th Bombing on Mitsubishi Works	34

Ⅳ. Why and how was Shizuoka bombed?
1. Why was Shizuoka bombed? ─ 36
2. Preparations for the Air Raid and its Execution ─ 38
   - Air Objective Folder　39
   - Map with area code　41
   - Litho-Mosaic　42
   - Photo-reconnaissance (pre-strike)　43
   - Target Information Sheet　43
   - Field Order　44
   - Photo-reconnaissance (post-strike)　45
   - Damage Assessment Report　46
   - Mission Summary　47
   - Tactical Mission Report　48

Ⅴ. Paintings and Photographs about the air raid on Shizuoka
1. June 20th Shizuoka Air Raid ─ 50
   - (1) Shizuoka city was burnt to ashes within a couple of hours　50
   - (2) People ran away in the storm of flames　52
   - (3) Heading the Abe River　55
   - (4) The day after "I am alive"　57
2. July 7th Shimizu Air Raid ─ 61
3. July 31st Ship's Bombardment ─ 63
4. August 1st-2nd Final air raid on Shimizu ─ 64
5. Bombing continued ─ 65
6. From the Ruined towns ─ 66
7. The Cenotaphs ─ 68

Acknowledgement ─ 70
References ─ 71

Do you know the meaning "Air Raid"?

I. What is an "Air Raid"?

「空襲」ということば 知っていますか？
I. 空襲とは？

I What is an "Air Raid"?
1. What's this photograph?

What town ／ city do you think this is ?

You might think that the photograph is of Kobe city after being hit by a major earthquake in 1995.

But, this town is not Kobe, Hiroshima or Nagasaki, but actually Shizuoka city, at the last stage of the World War II.

The city area was completely burnt to ashes in a single night by the massive U.S. fire bombings of B-29s on June 20th 1945.

This is what an Air Raid is.

Japanese charactor "Shizuoka" means "Peaceful Hills", where we can see Mt.Fuji.

---

1. 空襲とは？
1. この写真は？

この街がどこか，分かりますか？

1995年に起きた大地震の後の，神戸の写真にも似ています．

でも…この街は神戸でも広島でも長崎でもなく，第2次世界大戦末期の静岡です．

静岡の街は，1945年6月20日，アメリカの爆撃機B-29の焼夷空襲により，一晩のうちに焼け野原となってしまいました．

これが，空襲なのです．

「静岡」の意味は，「美しい岡」．ここからは富士山が見えます．

Fig.1   **The urban area of Shizuoka city after the Air Raid**

(Possession of National Archives and Records Administration / Courtesy of Yozo Kudo)

A few concrete buildings remain in a field of ashes. Hontori street runs diagonal from lower left to upper right in the middle of the photograph. The white part at the top of the photograph is the Abe River.

図 1.   **空襲後の静岡市街地** （米国立公文書館蔵 / 工藤洋三氏提供）

静岡の街は，コンクリート造りの建物がポツポツと残っているだけの，一面の焼け野原になった．
写真中央を左下から右上へ走っているのが本通り，写真上部に見える白い部分は，安倍川である．

2. "The Mean Point of Impact" was the intersection of Hontori street and Gofukucho street

Shoji Kobayashi followed his painful memory and painted the picture on the next page 40 years after that air raid.
At the time, he was a junior high school student.

    The building in the center is a well-known structure in Shizuoka.
    Do you know it ?
    Yes, it's the Bank of Shizuoka, which escaped the destruction of fire.

You can see many corpses covered in galvanized iron sheets on Hontori street.
At present, there are few people who remember these facts.

137 B-29 bombers were ordered to hit this intersection of Hontori street and Gofukucho street.
The aiming point is called **"Mean Point of Impact (MPI)"**

---

2. 爆撃中心点は，本通りと呉服町通りの交差点

この絵は，空襲から40年後，小林昭治さんがつらい記憶をたどって描いたものです．
当時，小林さんは中学生でした．

    中央に描かれている建物は，静岡ではよく知られている建物ですが，どこか分かりますか？
    そう，焼失を免れた静岡銀行本店．

本通りの道端に，トタン板をかぶせられた死体がたくさん転がっているのが見えます．
今ではこの事を覚えている人は，少なくなりました．

137機のB-29は，この本通りと呉服町通りの交差点に，焼夷弾を投下するように命令されていました．

この点は，「爆撃中心点(MPI)」と呼ばれています．

Fig.2   **Nakacho area in the morning following the Air Raid**

(Painted by Shoji Kobayashi, then age 15, 40 years after the air raid)

Fortunately my house was spared from the air raid. The next morning, I walked to the Nakacho area to see the area. There were many corpses lying everywhere covered in galvanized iron sheets. There were so many corpses near the rotary intersection that I could not move forward. The building saved from the fire is the bank of Shizuoka.

図2.   翌朝の中町付近 (小林昭治画, 当時15歳)
幸いわが家は焼け残った. 街の様子を見に中町あたりまで行く. 焼けトタンをかぶせた死体が あちらこちらに見える. ロータリー付近まで行くと, 至るところに焼死体が転がり, もう足が前に 進まなかった. 焼け残った建物は静岡銀行本店.

3. The dead are no longer seen as "human beings" but as "objects"

Nations fight wars.
But, every time, everywhere, it is the individuals who are wounded and killed by wars.

Individuals who were burned to death in air raids are no longer seen as "human beings" but as "objects"

---

3. 死人は，もはや人間ではなく物体に

戦争は国家間で起きるもの．
しかし，いつでもどこでも，傷つき命を奪われ，戦争の結末を背負わされるのは，個人です．

空襲で焼き殺された人は，もはや「人間」ではなく，「物体」になってしまう．

Fig.3   **The corpse of mother and child in the fire-fighting tank**

(Painted by Minoru Konagaya, then age 17, 40 years after the air raid)

Shizuoka city was burnt to ashes in a single night. There were a lot of charred bodies in the field of ash. I walked to Gofukucho street from my office at Shizuoka station. I saw the corpses of a mother and child in a fire-fighting tank in front of the present Parco store. There was no water in it. The mother embraced her child closely in her arms. I came to myself and recognized, "They were human beings!" when I looked at the mother's belly and noticed that it was the color of mackerel.

図 3. 　　　　防火用水槽の中の母子の死体（小長谷実画，当時 17 歳）
静岡の街は一晩で焦土となった．焼け野原にはたくさんの焼死体が転がっていた．職場の静岡駅から呉服町通りへ向かうと，現パルコ前の防火用水槽の中に母子の焼死体があった．水は蒸発して一滴もなく，母は子をしっかり抱いていた．焼死体を見慣れた眼には何とも思わなかったが，母親の腹部が鯖色をしているのを見て，はっと我に返り，「人間だったんだ！」と思った．

4. "The tears of Amida" recorded the blazing inferno

Can you imagine how hot people must have felt during the air raid?
There was a key to solve this question in *"Fukyoraian"*, located on the 100m east of the Mean Point of Impact (MPI), which survived the fire with its original specification intact.

"Fukyoraian" (Fig.4) is the private temple of the Watanabe family whose business started in the Edo era. They built the temple to hold a statue of Buddha – *"Amida"* in 1897 through 1915, which had been the property of the Emperor Kokaku, and was presented to the Watanabe family. Although *"Fukyoraian"* was wrapped in flames, the wooden carvings and outside columns remained. It is a cultural heritage. The lower half of the outside walls of *"Fukyoraian"* were constructed of "the Izu stone" (pumice tuff) and the upper half of stucco to ward off fire.

When I walked around the outside walls, I noticed a lot of black thin lines stemming from the small black patch within "the Izu stone" on the north, south and west side walls (Fig.5). According to Akira Watanabe, the master of *"Fukyoraian"*, these lines were the traces of the Shizuoka air raid. It seemed to me that *"Amida"* wept for the people in the blazing inferno.

Based on the microscopic observation and the X-ray diffraction analysis, the black materials are sulfur with black pigment. The melting point of sulfur is 120°C, and the viscosity suddenly increases at 160°C. According to the physical property of sulfur, I suppose that sulfur would begin to melt at 120°C and run down walls like thin lines, and fix on the wall above 160°C. Also, the wooden carvings and columns of the east side facing the courtyard remained, and the color of the wooden surface changed to blackish brown. In general, the wood begins to dehydrate and change its color to blackish brown at about 150°C, and burns at about 260°C. Therefore, we can assume that the east side of

Fig.4 The east side of *"Fukyoraian"*. The wooden cavings are escaped from fire (Coutersy of Minao Tabata)
図4. 不去来庵東側. 木彫などは焼失を免れた（田畑みなお氏撮影）

Fig.5 The master, Akira Watanabe shows many thin lines "Tears of Amida" on the north wall
図5. 北壁の細い筋「阿弥陀如来の涙」を指し示す当主の渡邉朗さん

Fukyoraian was heated about 150℃ to 260℃, which agreed with the 160℃ heating "Izu stone" mentioned above. If temperature of the wood and rock are heated above 150℃, the flames of higher temperature would be created.

Can you imagine running away from such raging high temperature flames?

The tree in Fig.6 is a gingko which survived the fire. The gingko and the other trees in courtyard were to protect *Fukyoraian*, (left side of gingko in photograph) from the fire. We can find some burnt deep cracks on the trunk of gingko, left as traces from the Shizuoka air raid.

"The tears of Amida" and gingko deeply remind us the Shizuoka air raids.

Fig.6 Gingko with traces of air raid protected *Fukyoraian* from the fire
図6. 不去来庵を炎から守ったイチョウ. 幹に空襲の痕跡がある

4.「阿弥陀如来の涙」が印した灼熱のるつぼ

炎に包まれた人々, どれ程熱かったか想像できますか？
この手がかりが, 爆撃中心点から100m東に建つ「不去来庵」にありました. このお堂は焼失を免れ, ほとんどそのままの姿で残っています.

不去来庵（図4）は, 江戸時代から続く豪商渡邉家の持仏堂です. 光格天皇の御念持仏・阿弥陀如来像を寄贈され, それを祀るために, 1897年から1915年にかけて建造されました. 猛火にさらされながらも, 外側の木彫や柱も焼けずに残った文化遺産です. お堂外壁の腰部は伊豆石（軽石流凝灰岩）, 上部壁は漆喰塗りからなり, 火災を防いでいます.

ところが外壁の周りを歩いてみると, 北・南・西の壁面には, 伊豆石中の黒い礫状物質から流れた, 多数の細い黒筋が認められました（図5）. 不去来庵の当主・渡邉朗さんによると, 静岡空襲の痕跡だということ. 灼熱のるつぼに呑み込まれた人々の惨状に耐えかねて, 本尊が流した「阿弥陀如来の涙」のようです.

この黒い物質を顕微鏡やX線回折で調べたところ, 黒い色素を添加した硫黄であることが分かりました. 硫黄の融解点は120℃で, 160℃になると急激に粘度を増します. この硫黄の物理的性質から, 伊豆石中の硫黄は, 120℃で融け始め, 細い筋となって壁面を流れ落ち, 160℃以上で壁面に固定されたものと考えられます. また, 庭に面した向拝の木彫, 柱などは燃え残っていますが, 表面は黒褐色に変わっています. 一般的に, 木材は約150℃で脱水反応が進み, 表面が黒褐色に変化, 約260℃で引火するといわれています. 向拝側はおよそ150℃から260℃に熱せられたことが推測され, 伊豆石が熱せられた160℃以上とも符合します. 石や木材の温度が150℃以上である時, 周辺にはさらに高温の火焔が渦巻いているはずです.

このような高温の炎の中に身を置き, 逃げる……想像できますか？

図6に写っている木は, 焼け残ったイチョウです. イチョウや他の木々は, 写真奥の不去来庵を空襲の猛火から守りました. このイチョウの幹には, 空襲で焼け焦げた深い傷跡が残っています.

不去来庵に残る「阿弥陀如来の涙」やイチョウは, 静岡空襲の姿を, 私たちに深く想起させてくれます.

**How Japan was before the Air Raid?
How was life during the war?**

II. Japan before the Air Raid

III. The road to the Shizuoka Air Raid

空襲前の日本は，どうだったのでしょう？
戦争中は，どのような暮らしをしていたのでしょう？

Ⅱ．空襲が始まる前の日本
Ⅲ．静岡空襲への道

II. Japan before the Air Raid
1. The Japanese bombers attacked Asian cities

The Japanese bombers had already bombarded a lot of cities in Asia and Australia before the air raids hit Japan.

During the first half of the 20th century, Japan participated in and initiated several wars. In 1931, Japan, having a plan to push into China, initiated the Manchurian Incident, which was used as an opportunity to start the so-called "15-year war" with China. The Japanese bombers attacked Jinzhou at that time. The Incident escalated into a full-scale warfare in 1937. After that, Japanese army and navy bombers conducted air raids on many cities, including Shanghai (Fig.7), Nanking, Chungking, Hankou, Lanzhou, and Kunming continuously. In fact, Japanese air raids were conducted against Chungking 218 times from 1938 to 1943. As a result, 11,885 people were killed (from the Chinese data).

The heavy army bombers attacking these cities stemmed from the corps organized in Hamamatsu, Shizuoka prefecture. The 34th infantry regiment and the 230th corps from Shizuoka took the war to various regions in China for the ensuing years.

Japanes navy bombers bombing Shanghai ("Weekly Photographic Magazine", August 10, 1938)

II. 空襲が始まる前の日本
1. 日本の爆撃機，アジア諸都市を爆撃

日本が空襲を受ける前に日本軍は，すでにアジアやオーストラリアの多くの都市を空襲していました．

日本は20世紀前半を，戦争に明けくれてきました．中国大陸への進出をもくろむ日本軍は，1931年，いわゆる「15年戦争」の引き金となる満州事変を起こしました．この時，日本軍は錦州を爆撃しています．中国との全面戦争となった1937年以降，日本陸海軍の爆撃機は，上海（図7），南京，重慶，漢口，蘭州，昆明など多くの都市を空襲しました．特に重慶に対しては，1938年から1943年までの間に218回もの空襲を行い，11885人の命を奪ったのです（中国側資料）．

都市空襲を行った陸軍重爆撃機の部隊は，浜松で編成された部隊が母体となったものです．日中戦争には，静岡県の歩兵第34連隊をはじめ，第230部隊などが投入され，長い間，中国各地を転戦しました．

図7. 上海を攻撃する海軍機
（「写真週報」1938年8月10日）

日本軍は,中国各地で,非戦闘員をも巻き込んだ戦闘を繰り返し,多くの住民に大きな被害を与えました.

中国本土での戦争は,年を追うごとに泥沼化していきました.この膠着状態を打開し,東南アジアの資源を得るために,日本は1941年,連合国側との戦争に突入します.この戦争は,現在,アジア・太平洋戦争と呼ばれ,第2次世界大戦の一部とされています.戦争の初期,戦況は日本に有利に運び,図8に示されるようにアジア・太平洋の広大な地域を占領しました.しかし1942年のミッドウェー海戦と,ガダルカナル戦での敗退の後は,次第に敗色の色を濃くしていきます.ガダルカナル島では,第230部隊の兵士の約80%が死亡しました.

戦局が悪化する中,アメリカ軍は1944年8月,マリアナ諸島を占領しました.この年の末,日本本土はマリアナ諸島の基地から,爆撃機B-29による空襲の標的となったのです.

図8.太平洋戦争時の日本の勢力範囲
戦争初期,日本の勢力範囲は拡がった(赤実線)が,終戦間際には大幅に縮小した(青実線)
(新編日本史図表,第一学習社,2004年より)

The Japanese army fought, dragging civilians into battles in every step of the way, and a large number of people were killed or injured.

The war on the Chinese mainland had been bogged down year after year. Japan opened war against the Allied Forces in December 1941, to change the situation and to get Southeast Asia's natural resources. At present, the war is called the "Asian-Pacific War", which is recognized as a part of World War II. The war went well for Japan in the early stages, occupying huge area in Asia and Pacific region as shown in Fig.8. But after the defeat in the Battle of Midway and the Battle of Guadalcanal in 1942, the shadow of defeat gradually emerged. In Guadalcanal, 80% of soldiers in the 230th corps died.

With the tide clearly turning against Japan, the U.S. Marines occupied the Mariana Islands in August 1944. Japanese mainland became targets of bombardment by the U.S. Army Air Force B-29 Bombers flying in from the bases on the Mariana Islands at the end of that year.

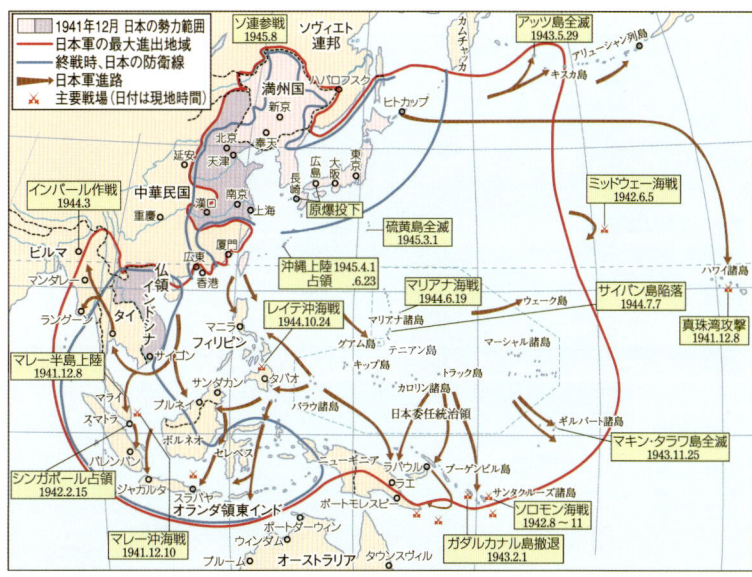

Fig.8　Japan's territory　　During Asian-Pacific War, Japan occupied huge area in the early stage (red solid line), but lost a lot of area in the last stage (blue solid line)
(After a new edited chart of Japanese history, printed in Daiiti-gakushusha, 2004)

2. The life of people in those days

As the war progressed, the industrial and agricultural production decreased remarkably, and the national economy was severely exhausted. The government enacted "the National Mobilization Law" (1938) and others. According to the acts, the government could mobilize all of human resources and material resources for the war.

The distribution of rice and daily necessities were controlled with coupons. The new block associations were organized systematically, and the ration, air-defense drill and others were managed through neighborhood. Most citizens could only get a little food and daily necessities.

Shizuoka, like the other cities of Japan, played various military roles during the war. We had the Shizuoka infantry regiment located in the ruins of the Sunpu Castle since 1896. There were many war industries converted from light industries. Mitsubishi Aircraft Engine Plant and the Sumitomo Light Metals Plant were relocated from big cities. A lot of men went to the front, as many students and young women were mobilized to work in such war industries or the farmhouse. Due to the lack of mineral

Fig.9　Collect Metals　According to the Collect Metals Law, many kind of metal goods were collected from each house. At the shoolyard of the Anzai national elementary school, Shizuoka city (Photographed by Ryuhei Yamanashi)

2．当時の人々の暮らし

戦争が長引くにつれて，農・工業生産は激減し，国民経済は大きく落ち込みました．政府は「国家総動員法」(1938年)などを制定し，人や物を戦争のために動員できるようにしました．

米や生活必需品は配給制・切符制となりました．新たに地域が組織化され，配給や防空訓練などは，隣組を通して行われました．市民は，食料も生活物資もわずかしか手に入らず，耐乏生活を強いられました．

戦争中，静岡市は他の都市と同様に，様々な軍事的役割を担ってきました．1896年に設置された静岡連隊は，駿府城跡に置かれていました．市内には，軍需に転換された多くの工場や，大都市から疎開してきた三菱と住友の工場がありました．大勢の男子が出征したため，学生，生徒や若い女性は，働き手を失ったこれらの軍需工場や農家へ動員されました．しかし，原料の金属資源も底をつき，図9のように，家庭から鍋や釜などの金属類が集められ，兵器などにつくり替えられました．

図9．金属回収
金属回収令により，各家庭から多種の金属類が集められた．静岡市安西国民学校の校庭で(山梨龍平氏撮影)

若者は学校で、軍国主義教育を受けました。教育の重要な目的は、天皇に奉仕する臣民を育てることでした。少年・少女は、体育の授業で、日本古来の伝統的な武道や、なぎなた（図10）を習いました。

学生以外の青年は、20歳になると徴兵検査を受け、兵役につかなければなりませんでした。戦争末期には、政府は学生を繰り上げ卒業させました。20歳未満で徴兵検査を受け、中には前線に送られた若者もいます。

また、14歳以上の多くの少年たちを、志願兵として入隊させ、あるいは満蒙開拓青少年義勇軍として、満州へ送りました。戦争は少年少女から、「子どもの時代」をも奪ったのです。

resources, many kinds of metals, including pots and pans from each house were collected (Fig.9) and remade into the weapons and others.

Young people were indoctrinated militarism in school. The important aim of the education was to earn to be good servants for the Japanese emperor. Boys and girls were taught Budo and Naginata (Fig.10) respectively in the physical education, which are traditional Japanese styles of fighting.

Young men reaching 20 years of age, except students, had to take a physical examination for conscription and serve in the army. At the last stage of the war, the government accelerated the graduation for students. Although they were under the age of 20, they had to take a physical examination for conscription, and some of them were sent to the front of the battlefield.

Also not a few boys, in spite of 14 years of age, were enlisted as volunteers, or sent to Manchuria as young soldiers. The war took away "childhood" from boys and girls.

図10. なぎなた体操
国民学校高学年の女子は、学校でなぎなたの授業を受けた。賤機南国民学校の校庭で（山梨龍平氏撮影）

Fig.10　Naginata lesson by girls　The schoolgirls of the upper grades were taught Naginata lesson in school. At the schoolyard of Shizuhata-minami national elementary school
(Photographed by Ryuhei Yamanashi)

III. The road to the Shizuoka Air Raid
1. The beginning of air raid over Japanese mainland

The U.S. Marines occupied the Mariana Islands in August 1944, soon afterwards, the airfields for B-29s were being constructed in Saipan, Tinian and Guam. To maintain attacks on Japanese mainland, the XXI Bomber Command was organized. It consisted of the 73Wing, 313Wing, 314Wing, 58Wing and 315Wing early in July, 1945. Each Wing had about 180 B-29s.

The newly developed B-29 at a huge amount of expense was called "Super fortress"(Fig.12). B-29 with 9 tons bomb load could fly more than 6,000 km and return to the bases after about 15 hours flight (Fig.11).

Recently, the outline of the air raids by the B-29 Bombers over Japan has been revealed using historical documents which are preserved at the National Archives and Records Administration (NARA) in the United States.

III. 静岡空襲への道
1．日本本土への空襲の始まり

アメリカ軍は，マリアナ諸島を占領するとすぐに，サイパン・テニアン・グアムに飛行基地を造りました．日本本土を爆撃するため，第21爆撃機集団を置き，1945年7月初旬までに第73，313，314，58，315の各航空団が配備されています．各航空団は，約180機のB-29を保有していました．

巨費を投じて開発されたB-29は，「超空の要塞」と呼ばれています（図12）．最大9トンの爆弾を積んで，約6000kmの距離を飛び，日本と基地の間を約15時間で往復することができました（図11）．

近年，B-29による日本空襲の概要が，米国立公文書館（NARA）に保存されている米軍の記録によって，明らかになってきました．

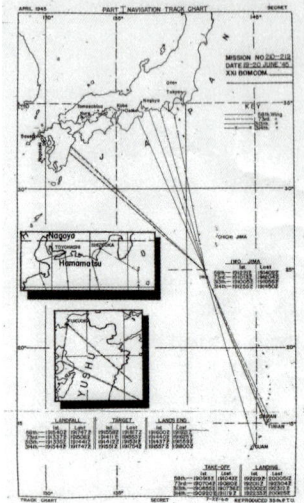

Fig.11　Navigation chart from the Mariana bases to Shizuoka, Toyohashi and Fukuoka
(Tactical Mission Report No.212, Possession of NARA)
図11．　マリアナの基地から静岡，豊橋，福岡への航路図
(作戦任務報告書No.212, 米国立公文書館蔵)

Fig.12　B-29 crew preparing bombs for a sortie at the base in Saipan
(Possession of NARA/ Courtesy of Yozo Kudo)
図12．　サイパンの基地で，出撃のため爆弾の準備をしているB-29搭乗員
(米国立公文書館蔵／工藤洋三氏提供)

The first finder of B-29 was a young man

The first flight of B-29 from the Mariana bases to Japanese mainland was on November 1, 1944. It was a reconnaissance flight.

Young men of the Inatori observation post, located on the south east coast of the Izu peninsula, kept watching over the sky using binoculars for enemy airplanes. They found a vapor trail over the Kozu-shima around 10:40 a.m., and caught sight of an airplane over Nii-jima. A young man, named Masahiko Suzuki (Fig.13), confirmed that the airplane was exactly a B-29 based on his knowledge from an illustrated reference book. But nobody believed him. The sub-chief of his post ran up to him and desperately said "If it would not be true, you should perform Hara-kiri." "Yes, I would.", he declared somewhat with anxiety, and reported to the head office immediately.

Next day, the newspaper reported the first sighting of the flight of B-29 and the great achievement of the Inatori observatory as a civilian air defense.

Fig.14 is the Matsuzaki observation post, same type as the Inatori observation post.

Fig.13 Masahiko Suzuki at present

第一発見者は青年

マリアナの基地から，B-29が最初に飛来したのは，1944年11月1日，偵察飛行でした．

この日，稲取（伊豆半島の東南海岸）防空監視哨の青年たちは，敵機を，双眼鏡で見張っていました．午前10時40分頃，神津島上空に飛行機雲を発見，新島上空で機影を捉えました．鈴木正彦青年（図13）は，雑誌に掲載されたB-29と断定，しかし誰も信じません．副哨長が血相を変えてやって来て，「もし間違っていたら，腹を切るか」と迫りました．鈴木青年は一抹の不安を感じながらも，「違ったら腹を切る」と断言し，この情報をすぐに上部組織へ通報しました．

翌日の新聞は，稲取防空監視哨が，初めてB-29飛来を発見するという快挙をあげた，と報じました．

図14は，松崎防空監視哨．稲取も同じ様な施設でした．

図13. 現在の鈴木正彦さん
図14. 伊豆半島南西海岸の松崎防空監視哨．哨員が望楼で敵機を監視している（斉藤只春氏提供）

Fig.14 Matsuzaki observation post, the south-west coast of the Izu peninsula
(Courtesy of Tadaharu Saito)

2. Three stages of Air Raid

The B-29 bombers began to attack the Japanese homeland from the base of the Mariana Islands on November 24, 1944, and kept bombing various targets, from heavy industries to local urban areas in Japan, until August 15, 1945. The bombardments by B-29 are, in general, classified into following 3 stages.

Stage I: November 24, 1944 to March 4, 1945. Main targets were aircraft industries, and precision bombing was made from high altitude using high explosive bombs. Damage was small. Fig.15 shows the B-29 Bombers heading toward Tokyo area.

Stage II: March 10 to June 15. Main targets were Tokyo and big cities. Incendiary bombs were dropped from low altitude at night. 7 big cities were reduced to ashes. When the XXI Bomber Command attacked Kyushu Airfield for supporting the Okinawa campaign, the strategic bombing was suspended for a while.

Stage III: June 17 to August 15. Main targets were small cities. 57 cities were burned by low altitude incendiary raid at night.

The bombings were continued on the military related factories and installations during Stage II to III. Oil industries were bombed at night during stage III.

Consequently, 27,000 B-29s dropped 160,000 tons bombs on Japanese mainland within 9 months. More than 400 of cities, towns and villages suffered by the air raid (Fig.20), and the total number of deaths is estimated to be 500,000 to 600,000.

B-29 pass Mt .Fuji, Japan en rout to bomb Japanese targets (Possession of NARA)

3. Tokyo Air Raid was the turning point

When the high attitude precision bombing attack became ineffective, Henry H. Arnold, the Commanding General of the Army Air Force, changed the Commanding General of XXI Bomber Command, Haywood P. Hansell to Curtis E, LeMay in January, 1945. LeMay believed that area bombing was necessary against Japan because urban areas were densely packed with a huge number of small household shops and wooden structures outlining area of the cities. He planned operations to burn down the centers of Tokyo, Kobe, Nagoya and Osaka with heavy incendiary raids at night at low attitude. The mission started from Tokyo.

Shortly after midnight of March 10, 285 B-29s dropped 1,665 tons of incendiaries over the density populated area of east Tokyo. The vast area became a blazing inferno in one moment, and was entirely burnt in a single night (Fig.16). More than 100,000 persons were killed in the raging wild flames. Two nights later, the huge aircraft production center of Nagoya was attacked. Soon after, Tokyo was severely attacked again in April and May, and about 50% of the urban area was destroyed.

Tokyo Air Raid on March 10 was the turning point of the air raid over Japan from stage I attacking mainly the aircraft industries to stage II of fire bombing the urban area.

Tokyo in the morning after air raid at 10:30 March 10 There were still smoldering over the burnt area (white part). The 3rd Photo Reconnaissance Squadron took Tokyo again next day for the damage assessment (Possession of NARA / Courtesy of Yozo Kudo)

Fig.17 The tornado of blazes
(Painted by Mitsuo Waki, then age 13, Possession of the Sumida City Museum)

The tornado of blazes in Tokyo Air Raid

Wrapped in flames, the storm of heated winds bellowed over the houses. The raging wild fire also burnt away many peoples, quilts and galvanized iron. Some people saw that a fire engine was rolling on the ground and blown 30 m away by the whirlwind of fire. According to the records of the central meteorological observatory, the wind was as strong as typhoon that blew over the fire area in the air raid on March 10 and May 25-26 (See p.29).

Fig.17 was drawn by Mitsuo Waki who watched the fire raid from the roof top of his house in Setagaya. He said "Suddenly tall pillars of fire rose. I watched 10 pillars in total. At first, I watched whitish yellow one which turned into reddish gradually, and disappeared. The next pillars of fire rose one after another, here and there every few minutes. I heard indistinct noisy sounds from the east. I couldn't imagine what happened under the pillars of fire. But I thought it over later, the noisy sounds like rumbling on the earth were the burning sounds of houses and peoples, also intermittent indistinct high sounds like women were all kind of voices-calls of family, cries, groan and wailing-of more than 100,000 peoples." [3]

東京空襲で見た火焔の竜巻

炎に包まれた地上には, 熱風の嵐が吹き荒れました. 熱風は人や布団, トタンをも吹き飛ばしました. 火災旋風が消防自動車を巻き上げ, 30m先に吹き飛ばしたのを見たという人々もいます. 空襲時の中央気象台の記録によると, 3月10日と5月25-26日の東京空襲では, 台風並みの風が吹いたことが分かりました(p.29参照).

図17の絵は, 脇三夫さんが, 世田谷の自宅の屋根から見た光景を描いたものです.

「突然高い火柱があがった. 私は10本くらいの火柱があがるのを見た. 最初に1本, 白っぽい黄色で, 次第に赤くなり, 消えていく. 2, 3分おきぐらいに次々にあちこちから立ちのぼっては消えていった. …東の方からかすかにざわめいた音が聞こえてきていた. …火柱の下で何があったのか想像もしなかった. 後で思えば, 火柱が立っている間, 聞こえてきた地鳴りのようなざわざわという音は, 家や人が焼かれていく音で, また弱々しく断続する人声のような高い音は, 10万余の人々の発するあらゆる声, 家族の呼び声, 叫び, うめき, 慟哭(どうこく)の集積音であったと思われてならない」脇さんの言葉です. [3]

図17. 火焔の竜巻 (脇三夫画, 当時13歳／墨田郷土文化資料館蔵)

空襲中の気温, 風速, 視程…が気象台で記録されていた

空襲は地上の気象をどんな風に変えたのでしょう.

東京の中央気象台の記録から, 次の事実が分かりました.

図18は, 空襲による大気の変化を表す, 典型的な記録です. 5月25-26日の東京空襲時(赤い範囲)には, 明らかに気温の上昇と湿度の低下が認められます.

図19は視程の変化. 空襲(赤い範囲)の後は, 東西南北方向の視程が低下しています. 東方向の視程だけは, 翌朝まで回復せずに低いままです. この事実は, 図16の煙が焼失域を覆っている状況を説明しています.

3月10日と5月25-26日の東京空襲では, 最大瞬間風速が, それぞれ
25.7m/秒(2:54)
30.0m/秒(0:40)
と記録されており, 台風並みの激しさだったことが分かります.

図18. 5月25-26日の温度と湿度

図19. 3月10日の視程
　　　　(工藤洋三他, 2009より)

Temperature, Wind speed, Visibility and others were recorded by the meteorological observatory

How did the air raid cause the change in the weather?

According to the records of the central meteorological observatory in Tokyo, we found out the following facts.

Fig.18 shows the typical records which exhibit the change of atmosphere caused by air raid. The temperature rose and the humidity remarkably fell down during the air raid (red colored) over Tokyo on May 25-26.

Fig.19 shows that the visibility in all orientations dropped after the Tokyo air raid on March 10 (red colored). The visibility in the east continued to be low to the next morning. This fact agreed with the smoke over the burnt area in Fig.16.

The maximum instantaneous wind speed in the Tokyo Air Raid on March 10 and May 25-26 are 25.7 m/s at 2:54, 30.0m/s at 0:40 respectively, which was as violent as in a typhoon.

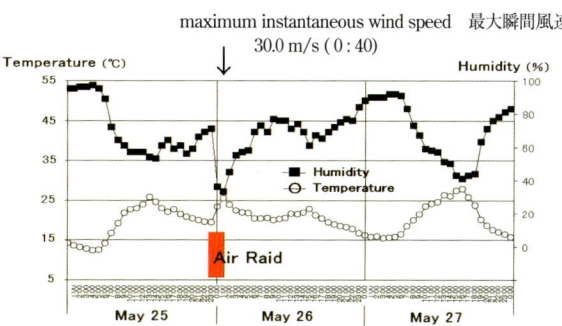

Fig.18　Temperature and Humidity on May 25-26

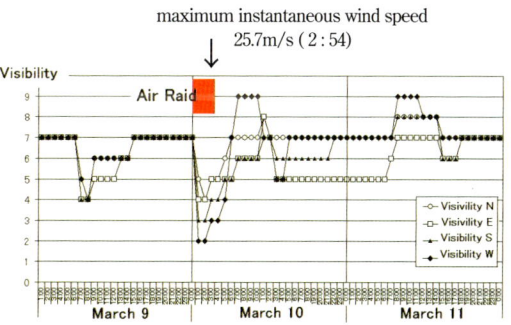

Fig.19　Visibility on March 10
(after Yozo Kudo et al., 2009)

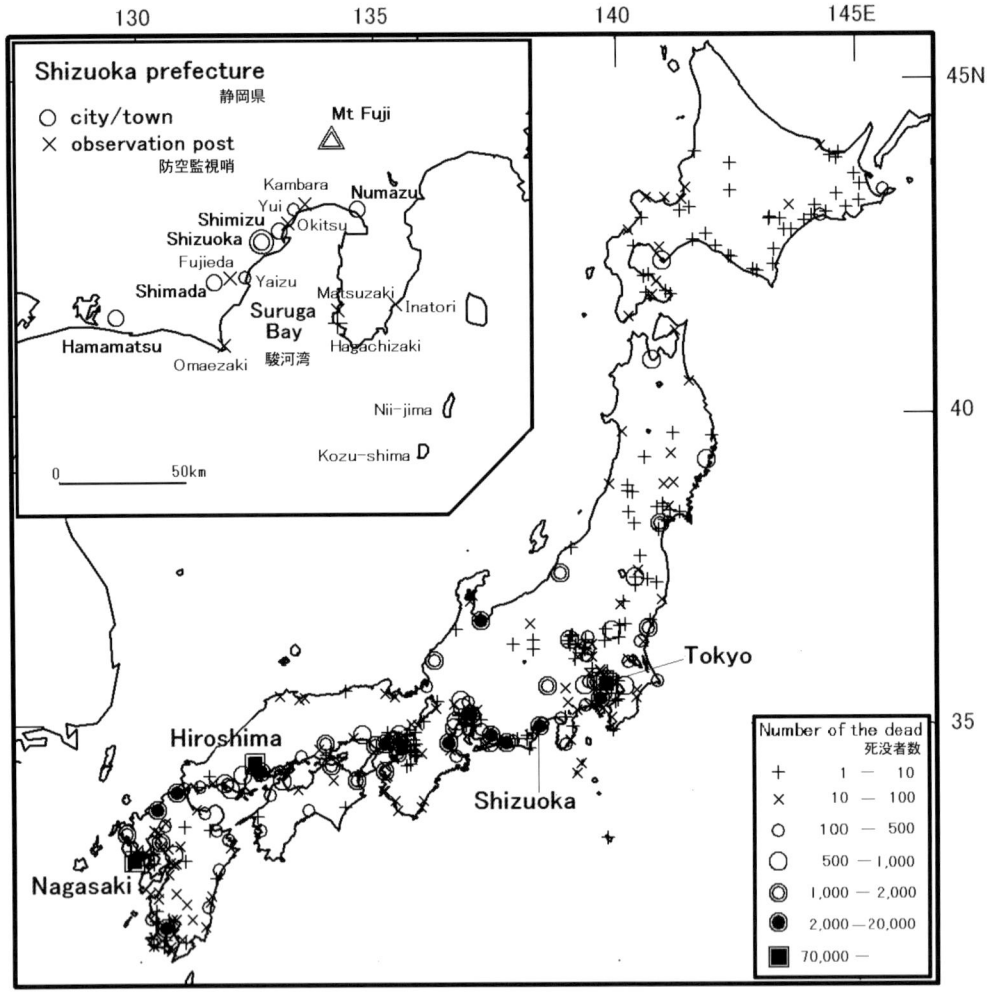

Fig.20 The disaster map by the air raid in Japan

図20. 日本の空襲被災地図

空襲の死没者を有する374の市町村を図示した. 広島と長崎は, それぞれ140000人と74228人である. 東京は115000人. なお, この図には海軍の攻撃による死者も含まれる.

地図の範囲を超える沖縄諸島や, 奄美諸島などについては割愛した. また空襲による死没者総数は, 現在のところ把握しきれていない. 全国にはいまだ, 地図上に図示されていない数多くの市町村がある.

資料は1994年8月14日付東京新聞などによる.

Fig.20 shows 374 cities, towns and villages with the dead by the air raids. The number of dead in Hiroshima and Nagasaki is 140,000 and 74,228, respectively. The dead number in Tokyo is 115,000. The dead by the naval attacks is also included.

While, the number of the dead in Okinawa Islands, Amami Islands and others isn't included because they are located beyond the scope of the map. Also, we cannot count the whole number of the dead at present. There are many other cities, towns and villages that aren't shown on this map.

Data is based on the Tokyo Shimbun (August 14, 1994) and others.

4. 静岡地域への空襲の概略

静岡は，駿河湾の西側に位置しています。北東にそびえる富士山が格好の目印となったため，東京へ向かうB-29部隊の通り道となりました。この地理的条件により，Ⅰ期からⅢ期までの，ほとんどのタイプの空襲や，海軍の砲撃を経験，計23回の空襲が記録されています。

全国各地の要所には，敵機の動向を見張る防空監視哨が置かれ，動員された青年たちが，24時間体制で監視していました（図21）。静岡県には70の監視哨がありました．

近年，飛行機の発見時間・機数・方向・高度などが記録された防空監視哨の資料が，静岡市周辺の藤枝と蒲原で発見されました（図22）．空襲体験者の記憶，米軍資料，米軍機を監視した資料，この3つから静岡の空襲を，客観的に理解することができます．

4. Outline of the air raid on the Shizuoka area

Shizuoka is located on the west side of Suruga Bay. Shizuoka was along the B-29 flight path en route to Tokyo where Mt. Fuji could be seen by heading North-east from Shizuoka as a good landmark to Tokyo. Because of this location, Shizuoka was bombed 23 times, and experienced almost all types of air raids and the Naval attacks from stage I through stage III.

A lot of air defense observation posts were established at every strategic point in Japan, where mobilized young men kept watch over the enemy airplanes round-the-clock (Fig.21). There were 70 posts in Shizuoka prefecture.

Lately, the historical materials of the Fujieda and Kambara observation posts around Shizuoka were found (Fig.22). These included the information of the enemy aircraft about the recognition time, number, direction, altitude, and so on. Therefore, we can objectively understand the air raids on Shizuoka area from three points of view – the memories of experiences about the air raids, the U.S. military documents and the records at the observatory.

Fig.21 Young men keeping watch on the enemy aircraft at Okitsu watch tower
(Courtesy of Tadahisa Ozawa)
図21. 興津防空監視哨で敵機を監視している青年たち（小沢忠久氏提供）

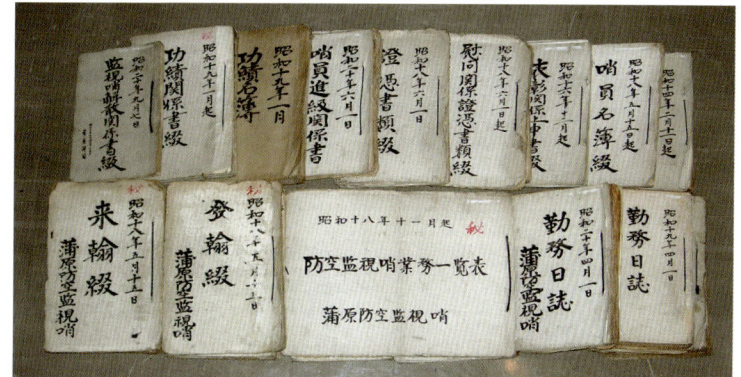

Fig.22 Historical documents related with air defense which were recorded at Kambara observation post and unusually preserved. Kambara is located on the east of Okitsu
(Courtesy of Aiji Mochizuki)
図22. 蒲原防空監視哨で，戦争当時記録された防空関係の貴重な資料．奇跡的に保存されていた．蒲原は興津の東にある（望月曖司氏提供）

Table 1 Time table of the air raid in Shizuoka area
表1　静岡地域における空襲年表

stage 期	year 年	date 月日	attacked area 被災地域	the dead 死者数	relationship to the attacks on Japanese mainland ** 日本空襲との関連
stage I 第Ⅰ期	1944	11.05	First flight of B-29 over Shizuoka 静岡地域への初飛来		photo reconnaissance 写真偵察
		11.27			on the way to the Nakajima AC.E in Musashino 中島飛行機武蔵製作所への往路 (以下中島飛行機)
		12.07	First fire raid/Naganuma/Shizuoka 静岡市への初空襲	unknown 不明	
		12.27	First bombing/Miho and others/Shimizu 清水市三保などへの初爆撃		on the way from Nakajima AC.E back to the Marianas 中島飛行機からマリアナへの帰路
	1945	1.09			on the way to Nakajima AC.E in Musashino 中島飛行機への往路
		1.22			weather reconnaissance 気象偵察
		1.27	fire raid/Ushizuma and others/Shizuoka 静岡市牛妻などへの焼夷弾投下		on the way to Nakajima AC.E in Musashino 中島飛行機への往路
		2.15	bombing/the Abe River/Shizuoka 静岡市安倍川への爆弾投下		on the way from Mitsubishi Aircraft Engine plant in Nagoya 名古屋・三菱重工からの帰路
		2.16			weather reconnaissance 気象偵察
		2.19	bombing/Yamazakishinden/Shizuoka 静岡市山崎新田への爆弾投下		on the way to Nakajima AC.E in Musashino 中島飛行機への往路
		3.04	fire raid/Kotobukicho and others/Shimizu 清水市寿町などへの焼夷弾投下	4	on the way to Nakajima ACE in Musashino 同上
		3.06	bombing/Nishijima and others/Shizuoka 静岡市西島などへの爆弾投下	5	radar scope photo mission レーダー写真撮影
stage II 第Ⅱ期		3.16			weather reconnaissance 気象偵察
		4.04	bombing/Kutsunoya and others/Shizuoka 静岡市沓谷などへの爆弾投下 Minatocho and others/Shimizu 清水市港町などへの爆弾投下	194	primary target was Mitsubishi AC.E in Shizuoka 第一目標：静岡三菱工場
		4.07	bombing/Kagoue/Shizuoka 静岡市篭上への爆弾投下	2	on the way to Nakajima AC.E in Musashino 中島飛行機への往路
		4.10			weather reconnaissance 気象偵察
		4.12	bombing/Mitsubishi AC.E Plant/Shizuoka 静岡三菱工場への爆撃	1	on the way to Nakajima AC.E and back 中島飛行機への往路・帰路
		4.13			photo reconnaissance 写真偵察
		4.24	bombing/Sumitomo Plant/Shizuoka 静岡住友への爆撃	26	on the way from Hitatchi AC.E in Tachikawa 立川・日立航空機からの帰路
		5.16	bombing/Kitayabe/Shimizu 清水市北矢部への爆弾投下		weather reconnaissance 気象偵察
		5.19	bombing/Chiyoda/Shizuoka, Shimizu 清水市千代田、清水市への爆撃	12	on the way from Tachikawa Army Air Arsenal 立川・陸軍航空工廠からの帰路
		5.24	fire raid/Anzai and others/Shizuoka 静岡市安西などへの空襲	37	on the way to Tokyo urban area 東京市街地空襲への往路
		5.26	fire raid/the Abe River/Shizuoka 静岡市安倍川への焼夷弾投下		on the way to Tokyo urban area 東京市街地空襲への往路
		6.10	bombing/Miho industrial area/Shimizu 清水市三保工場地域への爆弾投下	18	on the way to Japan Aircraft Co. in Tomioka 富岡・日本飛行機工場への往路
stage III 第Ⅲ期		6.20	fire raid/Shizuoka urban area 静岡市街地空襲	1952	2nd attack on the small cities 第2回中小都市空襲
		6.21			photo reconnaissance 写真偵察
		7.02			radar scope photo mission レーダー写真撮影
		7.07	fire raid/Shimizu urban area 清水市街地空襲	151	6th attack on the small cities 第6回中小都市空襲
		7.10			photo reconnaissance 写真偵察
		7.25	fire raid/Aluminum Plant/Kambara 蒲原町日軽金への焼夷弾投下		on the way to Petroleum Complex in Kawasaki 川崎石油コンビナートへの往路
	*	7.30	bombing from ship-plane/coastal area 艦載機による駿河沿岸への爆撃		Third Freet Task Force 38 第3艦隊第38機動部隊
	*	7.31	ship's bombardment/Shimizu 清水への艦砲射撃	44	ComDesRon 25 第25駆逐艦隊
		8.01	bombing/Shizuoka/Shimizu 清水・静岡市への爆弾投下	34	on the way from Petroleum Complex in Kawasaki 川崎石油コンビナートからの帰路
		8.02	fire raid/Miho and others/Shimizu 清水市三保などへの焼夷弾投下		on the way from Hachioji urban area 八王子市街地空襲からの帰路
			total of the dead 死者総数	2480	Shizuoka:2129 Shimizu:351 静岡：2129 清水：351

the number of the dead refers to the records of the U.S. Strategic Bombing Survey and others
* the naval attacking
** based on the materials of USSBS and record of Japan's observation post
"fire raid" means the incendiary air raid
"bombing" means the attacks by bombs
Nakajima AC.E in musashino means Musashi Plant of the Nakajima Aircraft Engine Works
Hitachi AC.E in Tachikawa means the Hitachi Aircraft Company Engine Works at Tachikawa

死者数は米戦略爆撃調査団報告書などによる
※海軍の攻撃
※※米戦略爆撃調査報告と日本の防空監哨の記録による
「fire raid」焼夷弾による攻撃を意味する
「bombing」爆弾による攻撃を意味する
Nakajima AC.E in musashino　中島飛行機武蔵製作所
Hitachi AC.E in Tachikawa　日立航空機立川工場

静岡への空襲は，本土空襲のミニチュア例

静岡へ最初にB-29が飛来したのは，1944年11月5日．それ以来，食べ物も着る物もない生活の中で，人々はいつ来るか分からない空襲の恐怖に，おびえ続けました．これまでに確認された空襲は，23回を数えます（表1）．

Ⅰ，Ⅱ期には，東京の中島飛行機武蔵製作所や，東京市街地へ往来するB-29が，途中で投弾した例が多く，9人が死没．

Ⅱ期の，4月4日の三菱静岡工場への爆撃は，目標を大きくはずれて，周辺の住民へ大きな被害を与え，およそ200人を巻きぞえにしました．また，5月24日夜中，東京空襲へ向かうB-29が，静岡市西部に焼夷弾を投下．安西地区周辺は火に包まれ，37名が焼死しました．市民は，初の本格的な夜間市街地空襲を体験します．Ⅱ期中には，合計で約290人の命が奪われました．

Ⅲ期は，夜間中小都市空襲で代表されます．静岡市は6月20日，第2回目の攻撃対象となり，その後清水市は，7月7日の第6回目の攻撃対象となりました．

続いて7月31日未明，海軍の艦砲射撃が清水市を襲い，大勢の人々が死亡しました．

翌8月1-2日には，八王子など4都市を狙った大規模な空襲の余波を受けました．Ⅲ期中には，約2180人の命が奪われています．

このように，静岡地域は，種々のタイプの空襲や，海軍の攻撃を受けました．日本本土への攻撃のミニチュア例と言えましょう．

Shizuoka-the miniature example what happened to the Japanese homeland

The first day of a B-29 flying over Shizuoka was November 5, 1944. Since then, fear of the air raid was added to the people who were suffering from hunger and poverty. We can confirm the 23 times of air raids on Shizuoka (Table1).

In Stage I and stage II, the B-29s dropped bombs on the Shizuoka area on the way to the Nakajima Aircraft Engine Works in Tokyo and its urban area or the Mariana bases. 9 people were killed during stage I.

In Stage II, the air raid against the Mitsubishi Aircraft Engine Plant Shizuoka works on April 4 missed the target. The bombs attacked a wide area and hurt many people. About 200 of citizen were killed.

B-29s dropped incendiaries (Fig.40) on the west part of Shizuoka city on its way to Tokyo urban area at midnight of May 24. The area around Anzai district was in flames, and 37 people were burnt to death. It was the first time that Shizuoka citizen experienced the real night incendiary air raid. About 290 people were killed during stage II.

Stage III is characterized by the mission of night incendiary attacks against the small cities in Japan. Shizuoka city was attacked in the second series of attack on June 20, after that Shimizu city was attacked in the sixth series on July 7.

Before long, Shimizu citizen experienced another violent bombardment again. The Naval ship's bombardment came at midnight of July 31. Many people were injured seriously.

Incendiary attacks against 4 cities including Hachioji on August 1-2 were in record-breaking massive missions. Shimizu was included in the air raid for Hachioji. About 2,180 people in total were killed during stage III.

As mentioned above, Shizuoka area was attacked by many types of air raids, and was bombarded by the Navy. We perceive the air raid of Shizuoka area was a miniature example of what happened to the Japanese homeland.

5. Before urban Air Raid : April 4th Bombing on Mitsubishi Works
test of the night precision bombing

Before Shizuoka urban air raid, on April 4, 48 B-29s dropped the flare bombs and the general purpose bombs over the foot of the Udo hill and the Shimizu area from 1:30 a.m. to 3:30 a.m. Nearly 200 people were killed. Mr.Y said as follows : [4]

"Suddenly the terrible sounds and vibration befell me. Although I didn't know what happened to me, I ran into the air raid shelter. Next morning, I saw unbelievable horrible scene beyond description. 16 persons who stayed in the shelter nearby scattered everywhere completely out of sight. Pieces of bodies and legs were hanging on the trees. Neighbors gathered up pieces of bodies which were buried in earth and sand under blown up houses, and then cremated the remains."

Also, Reiji Suzuki painted the experience in Shimizu district of Shizue Kuwabara, one of his friend in Fig.23. [5]

According to the U.S. Army documents, this mission was conducted by the 314 Wing against Shizuoka Aircraft Engine Works which was assigned to test a night precision bombing attack. Since this mission ended in failure, 11 B-29s of the 73 Wing struck again in daytime on April 12 and caused damage to the facilities. Also Sumitomo Works was attacked on April 24.

Fig.23
When I heard the air raid sirens, the big bombs directly hit our neighbor house. My mother and I were buried up to our necks. 9 neighbors were all killed
(Painted by Reiji Suzuki, story by Shizue Kuwabara, when they were 17 years old)

---

5. 市街地空襲前夜：
4月4日三菱工場への爆撃
夜間精密爆撃のテスト

静岡市街地が空襲を受ける前の1945年4月4日未明, 48機のB-29が有度丘陵の山麓一帯と清水地区に, 照明弾と一般目的弾を投下, 200人近くが死亡しました. 以下は静岡市沓谷のYさんの話です. [4]

「ものすごい音と振動で, 何が何だか分からないまま, 防空壕へ逃げた. 翌朝, 眼前に広がっていたのは, 言葉にできない光景だった. 近所の防空壕に入っていた16人は, 姿をとどめず周辺に飛び散っていた. 木に肉片や脚がぶら下がり, 吹き飛んだ家や土砂に埋もれた肉片を, 近所の皆で拾い集め, 荼毘にふした」

また, 清水地区の桑原静江さんの体験を聞き, 同級生の鈴木玲之さんが図23の絵を描きました. [5]

米軍資料によると, この空襲は, 三菱重工業静岡発動機製作所（略：三菱工場）を狙った第314航空団によるもので, 夜間でも精密爆撃が可能かどうかをテストする爆撃だったのです. この実験が失敗に終わったため, 4月12日の白昼, 第73航空団の11機は再び三菱工場を爆撃. 工場の施設に被害を与えました. また, 同月24日には, 住友軽金属プロペラ製造所静岡製作所（略：住友工場）が爆撃を受けました.

図23. 空襲警報が鳴った直後, 近所の家を爆弾が直撃. 気がつくと母親と首まで土砂の中に埋まっていた. その家は9人が全員亡くなった
（鈴木玲之画／桑原静江の体験, 当時17歳）

**Why was Shizuoka bombed?
How was it carried out?**

The answer was in the U.S. Military documents as follows.

IV. Why and how was Shizuoka bombed?

静岡は, なぜ空襲されたの？
どのようにして空襲されたの？

その答えは, 以下に示すように
米軍資料の中にありました

IV. 静岡はなぜ, どのように空襲されたのか

IV. Why and how was Shizuoka bombed?
1. Why was Shizuoka bombed?

We have been asked this question for a long time. Many people have believed "Because we had the Mitsubishi and Sumitomo works in Shizuoka." What's the true reason?

The answer was found in the declassified U.S. military documents. The document shows a plan with a target list of 180 Japanese urban areas to be attacked (Table 2). 180 cities were selected from the standpoint of population based on a census of 1940. From this list, they eliminated 7 big cities already bombed, and the cities proposed as the targets for the atomic bombs, the long-distance area — further north than Tohoku district. Focused on the remaining 137 cities, they analyzed some important factors for incendiary bombing, e.g. the congestion and the inflammability of a city, the city's relationship to the war industries, its transportation facilities, and the advantage of using radar bombing methods. Then, the attacks on small cities began with each raid of 4 cities from June 17.

One of the four cities targeted on the 1st night was Hamamatsu, and Shizuoka was targeted on the 2nd night, Shimizu was targeted on the 6th and Numazu was targeted on the 9th. One by one, these small cities were reduced to ashes. As a result, 57 small cities were bombed.

The description of the U.S. military documents is quite rational, though air raid victims tend to believe that their city had a particular importance to be attacked. Shizuoka was just one of the 57 cities for the U.S. Army. The reason why Shizuoka and Hamamatsu bombed in the early stage was that they were probably suitable cities for night incendiary attacks during the continued unfavorable weather condition. That is to say, they were not defended heavily, and provided a great advantage of radar bombing because of their locations along the coast and the congestion of the cities. Moreover, two cities were located on the main Tokaido Railroad.

These two missions were successful, and the radar bombing at night continued to August 15.

IV. 静岡はなぜ、どのように空襲されたのか
1. なぜ静岡は空襲されたのか

この問いを、私たちは長い間抱えてきました。「三菱と住友があったから」と、多くの人は信じてきました。でも、本当は？

その答えは、米軍資料の中にありました。攻撃目標都市を選定する資料となった180都市のリスト（表2）で、1940年の国勢調査を基に、都市を人口順に並べたものです。その中から、すでに焼いた7大都市、原爆投下候補地、遠距離の東北以北の都市を除く、残りの137都市にしぼりました。都市の密集性や延焼性、軍需工場や輸送機関との関連、レーダー爆撃の適否などの観点から、徹底した分析をしたのです。そして、小都市への空襲は、攻撃ごとにほぼ4都市ずつを組み合わせ、6月17日から始められました。

第1回目の夜間空襲の4都市の一つに浜松が、第2回目には静岡、第6回目に清水、そして第9回目には沼津が目標になりました。一つずつ、地方の小都市は焼かれてゆき、57都市が焦土となりました。

空襲された側は、特別な理由から空襲されたと考えたいものですが、米軍の判断基準は合理的でした。米軍から見れば、静岡は単に57都市の一つだったということです。ただ、静岡と浜松が初期に攻撃されたのは、梅雨時の悪天候下で、夜間焼夷空襲を敢行するには好都合の都市だったことが考えられます。つまり、防空が手薄、太平洋沿岸でレーダー爆撃に有利、都市の密集性が高いこと、さらに東海道本線の要所だったことを挙げることができます。

この2回の作戦は成功し、夜間のレーダー爆撃は8月15日まで続きました。

Table 2. 180 Japanese urban areas

3. Consequently, the first 180 Japanese urban areas (from the standpoint of population) were listed:

1. Tokyo	16. Kumamoto	31. Okayama	46. Ube
2. Osaka	17. Sasebo	32. Niigata	47. Aomori
3. Nagoya	18. Hakodate	33. Toyohashi	48. Fukui
4. Kyoto	19. Shimonoseki	34. Moji	49. Kawaguchi
5. Yokohama	20. Wakayama	35. Fuse	50. Akita
6. Kobe	21. Yokosuka	36. Toyama	51. Chiba
7. Hiroshima	22. Kagoshima	37. Tokushima	52. Morioka
8. Fukuoka	23. Kanazawa	38. Matsuyama	53. Kurume
9. Kawasaki	24. Sakai	39. Nishinomiya	54. Wakamatsu
10. Kure	25. Amagasaki	40. Takamatsu	55. Utsunomiya
11. Yawata	26. Kokura	41. Muroran	56. Asahigawa
12. Nagasaki	27. Omuta	42. Kochi	57. Maebashi
13. Sendai	28. Gifu	43. Himeji	58. Kiryu
14. Sapporo	29. Hamamatsu	44. Yokkaichi	59. Tobata
15. Shizuoka	30. Otaru	45. Kofu	60. Okazaki

61. Hitachi	91. Imabari	121. Niihama	151. Itami
62. Nobeoka	92. Matsue	122. Kamaishi	152. Kudamatsu
63. Oita	93. Numazu	123. Kuwana	153. Mishima
64. Nagano	94. Ujiyamada	124. Kamakura	154. Miyako
65. Hachinohe	95. Uwajima	125. Okaya	155. Saeki
66. Matsumoto	96. Odawara	126. Isezaki	156. Shingu
67. Takasaki	97. Komatsu	127. Tsuyama	157. Hagi
68. Ichinomiya	98. Hirosaki	128. Ashiya	158. Hamada
69. Yamagata	99. Iwakuni	129. Mihara	159. Kurashiki
70. Tsu	100. Funabashi	130. Tokuyama	160. Sakata
71. Shimizu	101. Saga	131. Kawajoe	161. Fukuchikyama
72. Otsu	102. Higashimaizuru	132. Yamaguchi	162. Yawatahama
73. Nagaoka	103. Tottori	133. Fujisawa	163. Tsuruga
74. Miyazaki	104. Handa	134. Obihiro	164. Karatsu
75. Mito	105. Kumagaya	135. Sanjo	165. Takayama
76. Suita	106. Yonezawa	136. Ishinomaki	166. Tochigi
77. Beppu	107. Onomichi	137. Higa	167. Shimbara
78. Kushiro	108. Ashikaga	138. Tsuchiura	168. Takada
79. Hachioji	109. Fukushima	139. Hikone	169. Taira
80. Nara	110. Wakamatsu	140. Tsuruoka	170. Nanao
81. Choshi	111. Akashi	141. Ikeda	171. Maizuro
82. Omiya	112. Yonago	142. Tamano	172. Kashiwazaki
83. Urawa	113. Nogata	143. Matsuzaka	173. Sumoto
84. Takaoka	114. Iizuka	144. Ueda	174. Nakatsu
85. Bofu	115. Kishiwada	145. Shikama	175. Kainan
86. Miyakonojo	116. Onoda	146. Kawauchi	176. Tateyama
87. Ichikawa	117. Seto	147. Noshiro	177. Iida
88. Koriyama	118. Toyonaka	148. Tachikawa	178. Marugame
89. Fukuyama	119. Isahaya	149. Nishijo	179. Tajimi
90. Ogaki	120. Hiratsuka	150. Yatsushiro	180. Atami

In this table, Shizuoka was No.15, Hamamatsu was No.29, Shimizu was No.71, Numazu was No.93, in order of population

表2. 日本の180都市　この表では人口順に，静岡は15番目，浜松は29番目，清水は71番目，沼津は93番目

2. Preparations for the Air Raid and its Execution

When and how did U.S. Army Air Force prepare for the air raid and carry out its execution on Shizuoka?

They placed historical officers at war theaters in order to report the useful information and preserve their accurate records.

Enormous archives which included many kinds of reports on every mission, important documents, various photographs and figures were preserved and administered in the National Archives and Records Administration (NARA). Formerly-classified archives are now in the public domain, based on "the freedom of information act." Japanese researchers on air raid, the National Diet Library and the research organizations have collected these archive, therefore many people can use them in Japan.

Based on the U.S. military documents about Shizuoka air raid on hand, we can understand that they had made careful preparations for the air raid for a long time, and learned lessons from all previous attacks and utilized them for the following attack. Here is a part of the plans and the operations about the Shizuoka air raid, in order of dating as follows.

1)	**Air Objective Folder**	1944
2)	**Map with area code**	1944
3)	Photo-reconnaissance	November 5, 1944
4)	**Litho-Mosaic**	February, 1945
5)	Urban Information Sheet	March 5
6)	**Photo-reconnaissance (pre-strike)**	April 13
7)	**Target Information Sheet**	June 14
8)	**Field Order**	June 19
9)	Photographs during strike	June 20
10)	**Photo-reconnaissance (post-strike)**	June 21
11)	**Damage Assessment Report**	June 25
12)	**Mission Summary**	June 28
13)	Tactical Mission Report	?

※ Numbered materials in bold letters are contained in this chapter. These archives are held at the National Archives and Records Administration (NARA). Photographs are provided by Yozo Kudo

---

2. 静岡空襲の準備と実行

米軍は、いつから静岡空襲を準備し、どのように実行したのでしょうか?

米軍は、役立つ情報を広く知らせ、正確な記録を残すため、戦域に戦史将校を配置していました.

作戦ごとの各種報告書、作戦に関連する重要文書、写真や図面など膨大な量の資料群が、米国立公文書館に保管されています. 当時の機密文書は、現在、公的な所有となり、「情報公開制度」によって一般に公開されています. 日本の空襲研究者、国会図書館や研究施設は、これらの資料を収集しており、誰でも資料を、国内で利用できるようになりました.

手元にある米軍資料から、空襲の準備は、長期間にわたって周到に進められ、空襲の結果を次の作戦に活かす方策も採られたのが分かります. 米軍の空襲準備と実行の一部を、順を追って紹介します.

1)	航空目標フォルダー	1944
2)	地域コード付地図	1944
3)	偵察写真撮影	1944.11.5
4)	リト・モザイク	1945.2
5)	市街地目標情報票	3.5
6)	偵察写真（空襲前）	4.13
7)	目標情報票	6.14
8)	野戦命令書	6.19
9)	空襲中の写真	6.20
10)	偵察写真（空襲後）	6.21
11)	損害評価報告書	6.25
12)	任務要約	6.28
13)	作戦任務報告書	?

※太字はここに収録している資料. 所蔵は米国立公文書館 (NARA), 写真提供は工藤洋三氏

1) Air Objective Folder   *prepared in 1944*

Fig.24 Air Objective Folder
図24.   航空目標フォルダー

The 20 Air Force set up the Joint Target Group in 1944. They compiled information on Japan collected before the war, and prepared a lot of materials based on them.

1) 航空目標フォルダー　1944年作成　空襲の前年, 第20航空軍情報部に統合目標部 (JTG) が置かれ, 戦争前に収集した資料を基に, 各地の情報をまとめて, 写真など多種の資料が作成された. これは一部. 図24の和訳はp.40

甲府90.16　静岡90.18　浜松90.21　の目次と概要

図24（P39）訳

航空目標フォルダー　　　　**静岡-清水-蒲原地域**　　甲府No.16-静岡No.18-浜松No.21 地域

目標No.	水力発電	ページ	目標No.	非鉄金属	ページ
1604	稲子水力発電所	10	1176	日本軽金属清水工場	8
			1177	日本軽金属蒲原工場	8

　この地区は，県都静岡および清水，蒲原を含んだ地域である．清水，蒲原は日本最大のアルミナ・アルミニウム工場として重要な位置を占めている．清水の日本軽金属アルミナ工場（目標No.1176）は，年間約100000トンの生産能力をもち，日本の生産の25％を占めている．この工場は，シンガポール地域からのボーキサイトをアルミナにし，ここから10マイル先の蒲原のアルミニウム工場（目標No.1177）や，本州北海岸にある新潟のアルミニウム工場へ供給するために建造された．

　蒲原工場は，アルミナをアルミニウムインゴットに還元する日本帝国最大の工場である．この工場は，2つか3つの電解槽室を持っており，それぞれ年間10000トンの生産能力を有する．大電力は同地内の50000kWの水力発電所から直流の電力が直接電解槽室へ導かれ，一般回線からの電力は工場内の整流器によって変換されて供給されている．水力発電の水はここから約10マイル北西から供給されており，そこには目標1604の45000KWの発電所がある．

　清水はこの付近では唯一の深い水深をもつ港で，大きな船舶の入港が可能である．比較的小規模の工場が市内またはその周辺に多数存在している．飛行機用の小型の電気部品を製造している小糸電気：富士電機（清水の直北）：ディーゼルエンジンを生産している伊藤鉄工：バッテリーを大規模に製造している日本電池：工作機械を製造するマルクニ鉄工などである．また，多くの缶詰工場，紡績工場や小規模な造船所などが散在している．これらの小さな工場は，目標としてリストアップはされていないが，偵察の参考として地図上に点示されている．三保半島に計画されている製油所については情報がない．

　長年，茶業の中心となってきた静岡市は，海に面しておらず，清水市の港湾地域とは東海道本線，電車や舗装道路で繋がっている．目標リストには載っていないが，マルクニ鉄工は唯一の大きな工場である．静岡市南東の郊外に住友と三菱の新しい工場が建設されるという未確認の情報がある．

　富士，大宮，岩淵など小さな町々は富士山の裾野，富士川の河口に分布しており，長年小規模な製紙業の中心であった．

　吉原や富士にはかなり大きなレーヨン工場もある．近年，この地域の水力発電の潜在能力が認識され，北部が広く開発されている．この地域のただ一つの水力発電所は，蒲原の北西にあるターゲット1604である．

図28（P43）訳

機内持ち込み禁止　　　　　　　　　**目　標　情　報　票**　　　　　　　目標：90.18－静岡

静岡　北緯：34°59′N　　東経138°23′E　　海抜：65フィート

1. 概要：静岡は，農業地域の生産物取引の中心地であるが，近年徐々に工業化が進んできた．東海道本線が通っており，鉄道の小規模の作業場がある．航空機の部品，紙，機械，発電や織物などを生産している．

2. 位置とその識別：静岡は東京の85マイル南西，駿河湾を西へ半分ほど南下した場所に位置しているが，市街地は海岸より3マイル内陸側に開けている．安倍川は街の西端を流れ，南方で駿河湾に注ぐ．東には丘陵が広がり，物資輸送の港を抱えた清水とを分断している．静岡の形状は不規則だが，南北約2.5マイル，東西約1.5マイル内に収まり，2つの丘陵の周辺の平野部に発達した街である．市の中心には古い城跡があり，攻撃上最も特徴的な目印となっている．

3. 目標の記載：静岡は，高度に工業化されてはいないが，約3.5平方マイルの中に，212198人が居住するコンパクトな街である．街の大部分は東海道本線の北方にあり，行政機関や軍関連施設が置かれている城跡などが密集している．静岡航空機エンジン工場（目標2011）は，かつて市内の最も重要な目標であったが，4月12日の爆撃でその86％を破壊した．先の爆撃で軽微な被害を与えた住友軽金属k.k.工場（目標2024）を含め，鉄道作業場，鉄工場，発電所，製紙工場，2件の紡績工場などがまだ存続している．1940年の火災時，火は急速に広がり6000戸の家を焼失させたという興味深い事例があり，静岡の燃焼性については既に証明済みである．平均人口密度は1平方マイル当たり60000人である．

4. 重要性：静岡は，横浜－名古屋間の太平洋沿岸にある最大の都市で，平時には日本茶の生産地としての役割を担ってきた．東海道本線沿線に位置することから，幾つかの軍需工場も誘致されている．

※以下は，掲載されていない次ページの訳

2011－静岡航空機エンジン工場－86％に破壊または被害を与えた．設備の補修または交換の努力は認められない．
2024－住友軽金属k.k.工場－生産物についての正確な情報はないが，恐らく飛行機部品，アルミ板であろう．清水や蒲原には，アルミの大供給源がある．
東洋紡績工場　　三光紡績工場－これらは軍需工場に転換されているだろう．
小黒弾薬庫　　　製紙工場　　　マルクニ鉄工　　静岡鉄道作業場　　ガス工場　　発電所

5. 照準点：照準点は，野戦命令書に記す．

1945年6月14日　第21爆撃機集団A-2情報部，目標班

2) Map with area code   *prepared in 1944*

Fig.25 shows the area code map prepared by the Joint Target Group. In this map, Japan was divided into 39 areas. For example;

Shizuoka area　：90.18
Izu Islands　　 ：90.19
Hamamatsu area：90.20

The number of 90 means the country code of Japan. The next number 18 through 20 means the area code.

2) 地域コード付地図
　　1944年作成

　図25は，統合情報部によって作成された地域コードを記した地図．日本は図のように39の地域に分けられた．例えば，

静岡地域は　　90.18
伊豆地域は　　90.19
浜松地域は　　90.20

　90は，国別番号で日本本土を示しており，次の18から20の数字は地域コード．

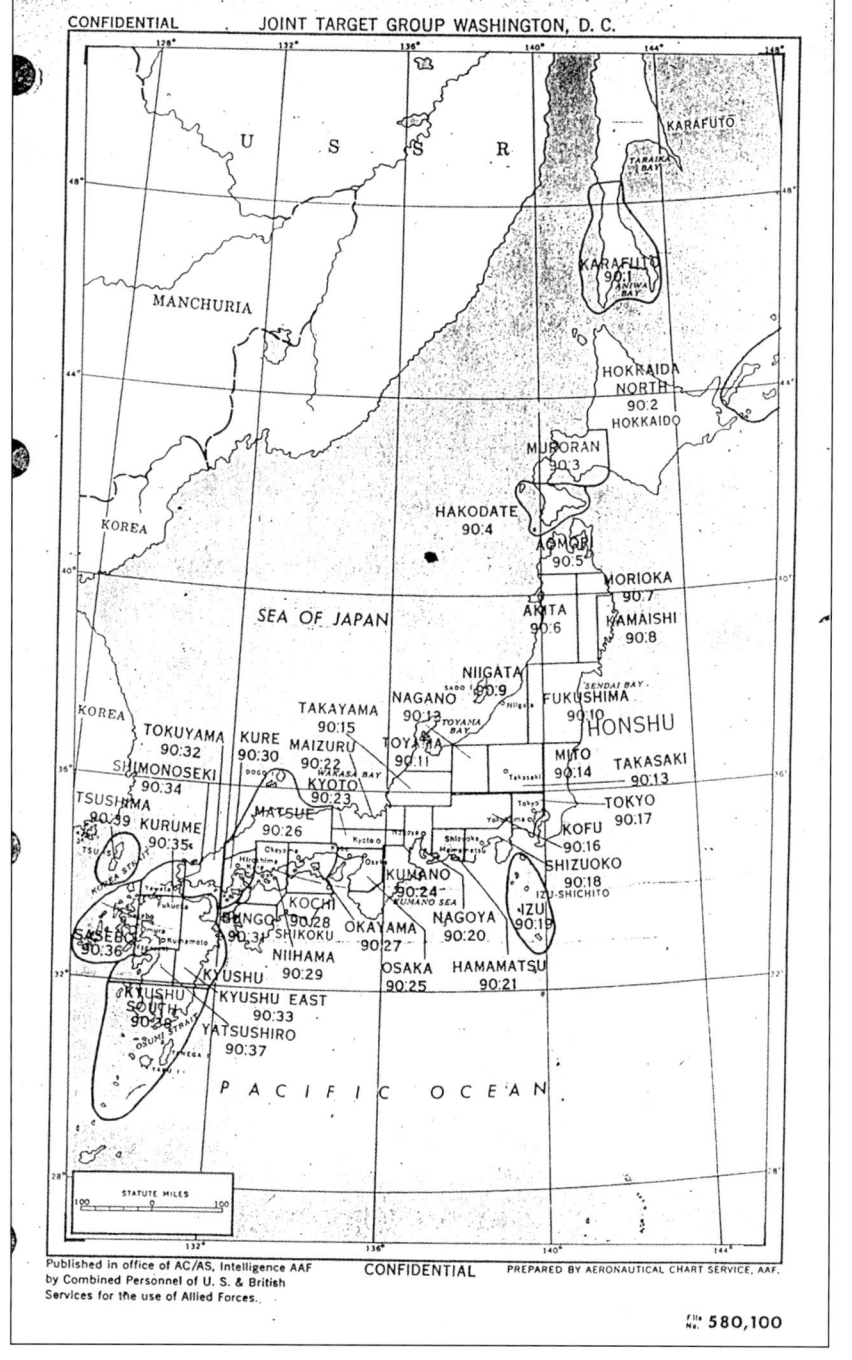

Fig.25　　Map with area code
図25.　　地域コード付地図

41

4) Litho-Mosaic   prepared in February, 1945

Fig.26   Litho・Mosaic
図26.   リト・モザイク

  The picture listed above is called "Litho-Mosaic". This mosaic was used for the reference of aiming point (AP) or mean point of impact (MPI).   With this mosaic the crew of B-29 studied the exact AP or MPI. All bombers were supposed to bomb the designated point. It was prepared by the A2 section of the XXI Bomber Command Headquarters. Printed mosaics were cut into squares with each side measuring 38.5 cm, and marked the scale on all sides. With this scale, the coordinates of AP or MPI was given to bombardiers.   MPI of Shizuoka was 045106 (045: the abscissa, 106: the ordinate). The point designated by the litho-mosaic located on the intersection of Hontori street and Gofukucho street. On this litho-mosaic, a circle with its center equal to MPI and a radius in 1.2km are drawn. This circle is called "circular error probability". It was expected that Shizuoka would be in ruins if half of gross bombs hit within the circle. In practice, the important part of the urban area was within the circle, and designated MPI was in the center of the urban area.

---

4) リト・モザイク　1945年2月作成

 上の図は「リト・モザイク」と呼ばれる．攻撃目標の照準点(AP)や爆撃中心点(MPI)の参照用として用いられ，B-29の搭乗員はこのモザイクからAPやMPIの正確な位置を知った．すべての爆撃機は，指定されたこの点を爆撃するよう求められていた．第21爆撃機集団司令部のA2情報部による作成．モザイクは1辺38.5ｃｍの正方形に切り取られ，4辺に目盛りが付されているので，爆撃手はAPやMPIを縦横の座標で読むことができた．静岡のMPIは，045106 (045：横軸，106：縦軸) で，本通りと呉服町通りの交差点．図中にMPIを中心とする半径1.2ｋｍの円が描かれているが，これは「確率誤差円」と呼ばれており，米軍はこの円の中に焼夷弾の半量が落ちれば，静岡の主要部分は壊滅すると考えていた．実際，市街地の重要部分はこの円内にあり，指定されたMPIは市街地の中心にあった．

6) Photo-reconnaissance (pre-strike)   1945.4.13

This photograph was taken by the 3rd Photo Reconnaissance Squadron on April 13 in preparation for attack on Shizuoka urban area. The diamond-shaped part in the center is the ruins of the Sunpu Castle. The whitish part of lower right is Mitsubishi works which were bombed the day before. The white part in left end is the Abe River.

6) 偵察写真（空襲前） 1945年4月13日

この写真は，静岡市街地への空襲の準備として，4月13日，第3写真偵察隊によって撮影されたもの．中央に見える菱形は駿府城跡．右下の白い部分は前日爆撃された三菱工場．左端の白い部分は，安倍川．

Fig.27　Pre-strike photograph of Shizuoka city
図27.　空襲前の静岡市の偵察写真

7) Target Information Sheet   1945.6.14

Before taking off for bombing mission, there was a briefing. Target Information Sheet which was described the latest information of Shizuoka was used to encourage the crew. A warning message "not to be taken into the air on combat missions" can be seen.

7) 目標情報票　1945年6月14日

出撃前に司令部はブリーフィングを行う．目標情報票には，静岡の最新情報が記載されており，爆撃手に目的意識を持たせ，戦意を高めるために使われた．「機内への持ち込みは禁止」と記されている．図28の和訳はp.40参照．

Fig.28　Target Information Sheet
図28.　目標情報票

8) Field Order　　1945.6.19

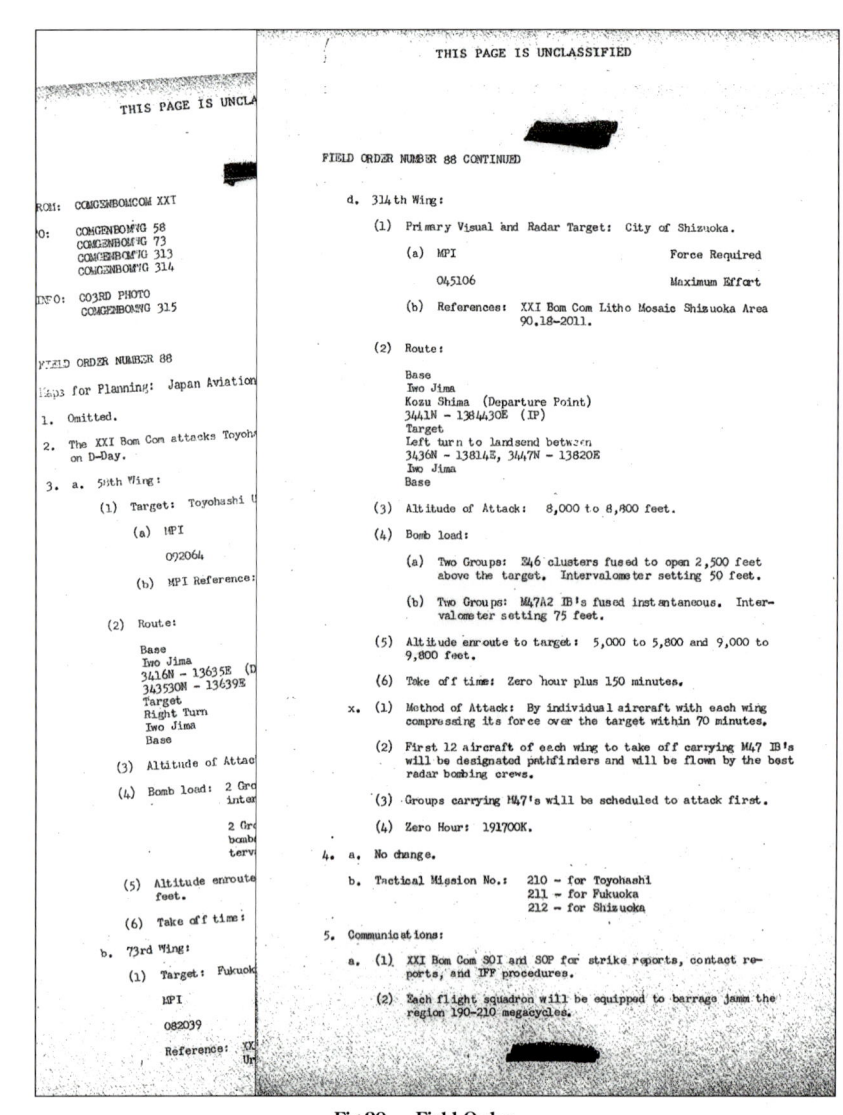

Fig.29　Field Order
図29.　野戦命令書

On the D-day, the Headquarters of XXI Bomber Command ordered a sally to 4 wings

8) 野戦命令書　1945年6月19日
　出撃当日，第21爆撃機集団司令部が，攻撃命令として作戦任務の内容を配下の4航空団に発した．

野戦命令第88号　第21爆撃機集団は，豊橋・福岡・静岡の市街地を攻撃する（以下静岡のみ抄訳）
d. 314航空団　**(1)** 目視およびレーダーによる第1目標：静岡市 (a) MPI　045106　最大努力 (b) 参照：第21爆撃機集団リト・モザイク静岡地域 90.18-2011　**(2)** 航路：基地－硫黄島－神津島（発進開始点）－北緯34°41′（攻撃始点）－目標左旋回－離岸点〔北緯34°36′東経138°14′と北緯34°47′東経138°20′の間〕－硫黄島－基地　**(3)** 攻撃高度：8000～8800フィート　**(4)** 搭載爆弾：(a) 2箇群団：E46集束焼夷弾－目標上空2500フィートで解束する信管付き．投下間隔は50フィートに設定 (b) 2箇群団：M47A2焼夷爆弾－瞬発弾頭信管付き．投下間隔75フィートに設定　**(5)** 目標までの飛行高度 5000～5800 および 9000～9800フィート　**(6)** 離陸時間：最初の機はゼロ時刻より150分遅く離陸すること　X. (1) 攻撃法：それぞれの航空団は目標への攻撃を70分以内に圧縮する (2) 優秀なレーダー爆撃手による最初の12機は先導機として M47 を投下 (3) M47を搭載している群団は早期に攻撃する (4) ゼロ時刻：19日16時（日本時間 ※通信妨害は省略）

10) Photo reconnaissance (post-strike)　　1945.6.21

Fig.30　　**Post-strike photograph of Shizuoka city**
図30.　　空襲後の静岡市の偵察写真

This photograph was taken by the 3rd Photo Reconnaissance Squadron on the following day of Shizuoka air raid. The white part is the burnt out area. A line running right to left at the central part of the photograph is the Tokaido railroad line. The Abe River is along the left-hand side. The diamond-shaped part near the center is the ruins of the Sunpu Castle where the Shizuoka infantry regiment was located. The burnt out area mainly spread all over the built-up area north of the Tokaido railroad line.

10) 偵察写真（空襲後） 1945年6月21日
　　第3写真偵察隊が空襲翌日に撮影した写真. 白く見える部分は焼失した地域. 中央左右に走っている線は東海道本線. 左側の白い帯状は安倍川. 中央近くに見える菱形部分は駿府城跡. 中に静岡歩兵連隊が置かれていた. 焼失域は, 主に東海道本線北側の住宅密集地に大きな拡がりを見せている.

11) Damage Assessment Report　　　1945.6.25

```
                          CONFIDENTIAL
                            C.I.U.
                       XXI BOMBER COMMAND
                       APO 234, c/o POSTMASTER
                       SAN FRANCISCO, CALIFORNIA

   (Combined PI Sections: 3rd Photo Recon Sqdrn and 35th Photo Tech Unit)

                                                25 June 1945

                   DAMAGE ASSESSMENT REPORT NO. 98

   Mission No.: XXI Bom Com 212       Target Area: Shizuoka (90.18)

   Date Flown: 19 June 1945

                            SUMMARY

       Damage to the city of Shizuoka resulting from XXI Bom
   Com Mission 212, 19 June 1945, totals 2.25 sq. mi., which
   represents about 66% of the entire city.

       Target 90.18-2024, the only numbered industrial target to
   be affected, was severely damaged. Seven buildings, about
   594,660 sq. ft., were destroyed. This represented about
   76.5% of the plant's total roof area.

       Damage to unnumbered targets was as follows: (Numbers used
   here correspond to those appearing in Ref. A):

            9. Toyo Textile Mill - slight damage.
           14. Gas Works - destroyed.
           15. Shizuoka RR Yards & Shops - damaged, and many small
                                           buildings destroyed.
           16. Shizuoka Castle Infantry Barracks - damaged.
           18. Light industrial district - destroyed.
           20. Probable Textile Mill - damaged.
           21. New residential and commercial construction -
                                                 destroyed.

       Old damage to Shizuoka totals about 1,210,000 sq. ft.

       Total damage to the city is 63,562,652 sq. ft. (2.28 sq. mi.;
   1460 acres) which represents 66% of the entire city.

   References:    A. J. T. G. Information, 90.18-2024-TL, 16 May 1945
                  B. CIU Damage Assessment Report 76

   Inclosures:    1. Mosaic showing damage to Shizuoka city.
                  2. Diagram showing damage to Shizuoka city.
                  3. Post-strike mosaic from 3PR5M287-2: 72, 73

                              Approved ..................
                                   HAMILTON D. DARBY,
                                   MAJOR, AC

   DISTRIBUTION B

                          CONFIDENTIAL
```

秘密
第21爆撃機集団 中央情報局 1945.6.25
　　損害評価報告書　第98号
任務番号：212　目標：静岡（90.18）　1945.6.19
　　　　　要約
　1945年6月19日の第21爆撃機集団作戦任務番号212による静岡市への爆撃によって与えた損害は，2.25平方マイル．これは市街地の66％に相当する．唯一番号が付けられた90.18-2024は，大きな被害を受けた．7棟の建物，約594660平方フィートが破壊されたが，これは全屋根面積の76.5％に当たる．番号が付けられていない目標の被害は以下の通り（ここで使用された番号は，参照Aに対応する）：
 9. 東洋紡績－軽微な損害
14. ガス工場－破壊
15. 静岡操車場および作業場－被害，および小さな建物が破壊
16. 静岡城跡内の歩兵連隊兵舎－被害
18. 軽工業地域－破壊
20. おそらく紡織工場－破壊
21. 新規建造の住宅と商業施設－破壊
　この空襲以前の損害は約1210000平方フィート．損害合計は63562652平方フィート（2.25平方マイル：1460エーカー）．これは市全体の66％に相当する．
参照　A. 統合目標グループ情報，
　　　　90.18-2024-TL，1945.5.16
　　　B. 中央情報局，損害評価報告76号
同封　1. 静岡市の損害を示すモザイク
　　　2. 静岡市の損害を示す図
　　　3. 第3写真偵察隊5M287-2からの空襲後のモザイク：72，73
承認　空軍少佐 Hamilton D. Darby

Fig.31-1　Damage Assessment Report
図31-1.　損害評価報告書

C.I.U. reported the damage assessment to the XXI Commanding General after the comparison of the photograph between pre-strike and post-strike.

11) 損害評価報告書　1945年6月25日
　中央情報局は，静岡への空襲前・後の偵察写真を比較・分析し，損害の概要を記した損害評価報告書を第21爆撃機集団司令官へ提出した．

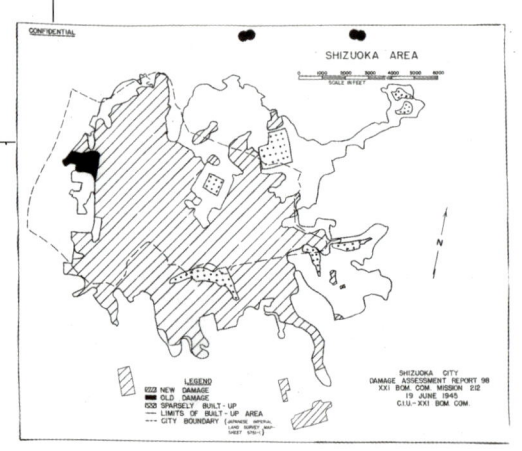

Fig.31-2　Diagram showing damage to Shizuoka city
図31-2.　静岡市の損害を示す図

12) Mission Summary　　　1945.6.28

```
                    S E C R E T
                   MISSION SUMMARY
            Mission Number 212     28 June 1945

   1. Date: 19 June 1945
   2. Target: Shizuoka Urban Area (90.18)
   3. Participating Unit: 314th Bombardment Wing
   4. Number A/C Airborne: 137
   5. % A/C Bombing Primary: 91.25% (125 primary and 1 opportunity)
   6. Type of Bombs and Fuzes: E-46 500 lb. incendiary clusters
                               set to open 2500' above target and
                               AN-M47A2 100 lb. incendiary bombs
                               with instantaneous nose.
   7. Tons of Bombs Dropped: 868.3 tons on primary and 9.6 tons
                              on opportunity.
   8. Time Over Primary: 0151K - 0354K
   9. Altitude of Attack: 8000 - 12,000 feet
  10. Weather Over Target: 0/10 - 2/10
  11. Total A/C Lost: 2
  12. Resume of Mission: Main portion of city destroyed. Damage
      totaled 2.28 sq. miles or 66% of built-up portion of city. Eighteen
      E/A sighted made 4 attacks. Light, medium and heavy flak, meager to
      moderate, generally inaccurate. Several S/L observed. Both B-29's
      were lost to unknown reasons. Eleven A/C were non-effective. Two
      B-29's landed at Iwo Jima. Average bomb load: 15,078 lbs. Average
      fuel reserve: 954 gallons.




                    S E C R E T
```

Fig.32　Mission Summary
図32．任務要約

The Command of the 314 Wing submitted a mission summary to the XXI Bomber Command as fast as possible

> **12) 任務要約**　1945年6月28日
> 　314航空団が基地に着いた後，できるだけ早く第21爆撃機集団司令官へ提出した任務要約

秘密
任務要約

任務番号212　　　1945.6.28

1. 日付　1945年6月19日
2. 目標：静岡市街地（90.18）
3. 参加単位：314航空団
4. 出撃機数：137機
5. 第1目標爆撃機：91.25%
   （第1目標125機／臨機1機）
6. 爆弾と信管の種類：
   目標上空2500フィートで解束するよう設定したE46-500ポンド集束焼夷弾およびAN-M47A2-100ポンド焼夷爆弾
7. 投下爆弾量：第1目標に868.3トン，臨機目標に9.6トン
8. 第1目標上空時間：
   0時51分－2時54分（日本時間）
9. 攻撃高度：
   8000－12000フィート
10. 目標上空の天気：0/10－2/10
11. 損失機合計：2機
12. 任務の要約：
    静岡市内の主要な部分は破壊された．全損害は2.28平方マイルでこれは建物密集地の66%に当たる．18機の敵機による攻撃を4回受ける．軽，中および重高射砲による対空砲火は貧弱ないし中程度で，概して不正確だった．探照灯が幾つか観察された．2機のB-29が失われたが原因は不明．11機が無効．2機のB-29が硫黄島に着陸．爆弾の平均搭載量は15078ポンド，燃料平均残量は954ガロン．

13) Tactical Mission Report

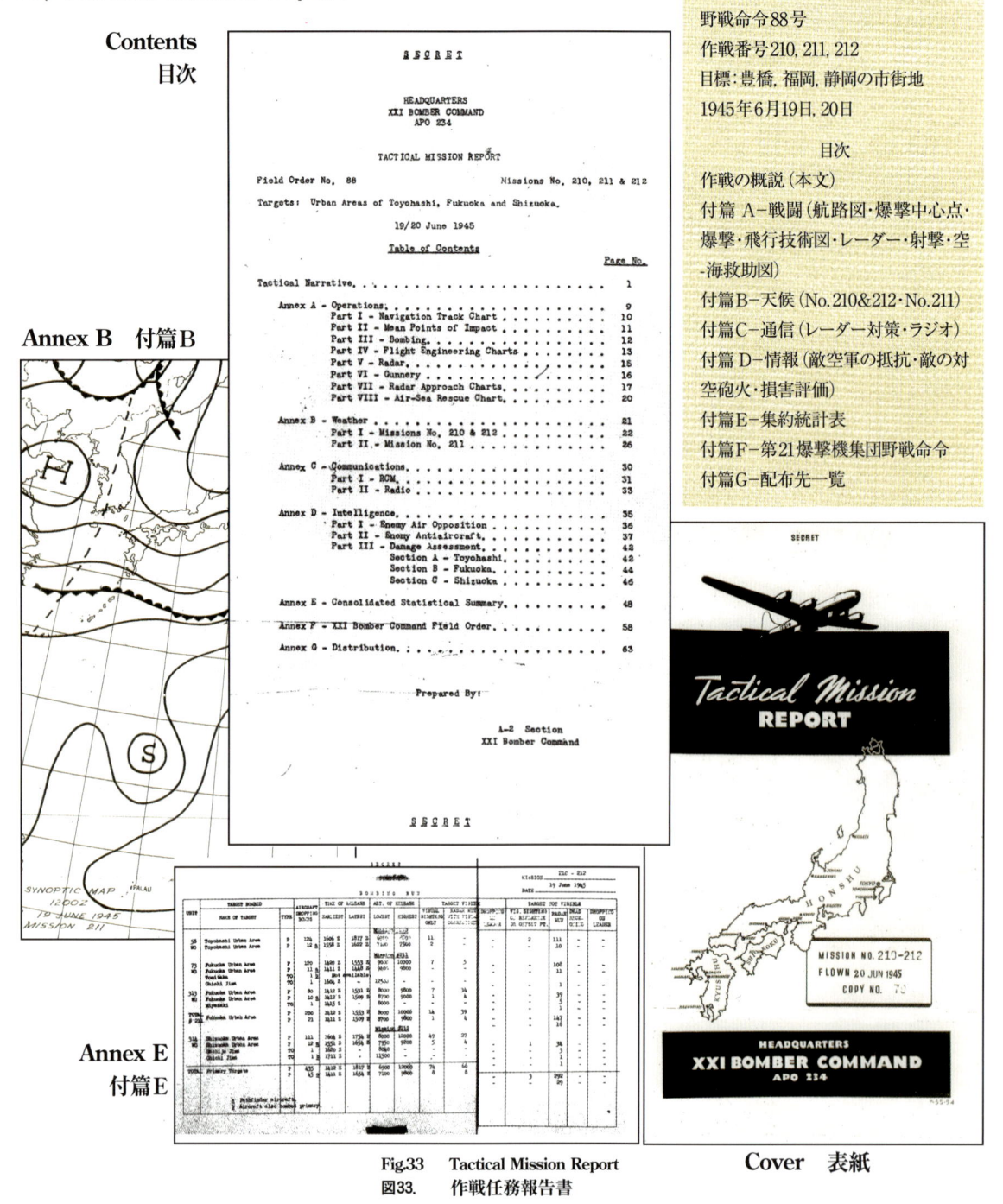

Contents 目次

Annex B　付篇B

Annex E　付篇E

作戦任務報告書
野戦命令88号
作戦番号210, 211, 212
目標：豊橋, 福岡, 静岡の市街地
1945年6月19日, 20日

目次
作戦の概説（本文）
付篇A－戦闘（航路図・爆撃中心点・爆撃・飛行技術図・レーダー・射撃・空・海救助図）
付篇B－天候（No.210＆212・No.211）
付篇C－通信（レーダー対策・ラジオ）
付篇D－情報（敵空軍の抵抗・敵の対空砲火・損害評価）
付篇E－集約統計表
付篇F－第21爆撃機集団野戦命令
付篇G－配布先一覧

Cover　表紙

Fig.33　Tactical Mission Report
図33.　作戦任務報告書

Tactical Mission Report was the final report which was submitted from XXI Bomber Command to the 20th Air Force
13) **作戦任務報告書**　第21爆撃機集団司令部から第20航空軍司令官への個々の作戦の最終報告書

48

What happened to people in Shizuoka?

People drew Pictures 40 years after air raid.
Photographs taken by U.S. Army were found.
These told about the air raid that night.

V. Paintings and Photographs about the air raid on Shizuoka

その時，人々に何が？

人々が40年を経て描いた絵．
あの時米軍が撮った写真は，
あの空襲を語ってくれる…

V. 絵と写真が語る静岡の空襲

V. Paintings and Photographs about the air raid on Shizuoka
1. June 20th Shizuoka Air Raid
(1) Shizuoka city was burnt to ashes within a couple of hours

Suddenly, incendiary cluster (Fig.39) dropped upon the sleeping people. Many people ran away desperately from the raging wild flame which burned many houses and people. Some of them remembered the painful memories and painted or wrote them with deep desire for peace. According to the paintings, notes and photographs, we will remember the Shizuoka Air Raid.

The 314Wing passed over Hagachizaki, Izu peninsula at midnight of June 20, started sweeping from the coast to the center of city. 123 B-29s dropped 868 tons of incendiaries from 0:51 a.m. through 2:54 a.m., and 66% of built-up area in Shizuoka was damaged (Fig.42,46).

Just before the air raid siren, incendiary bombs were dropped around the Shizuoka station. An aerial photograph of Fig.34 was taken from a B-29 during the bombing. Soon after the beginning of the attack, the central part of the city was already wrapped in flames. Shizuoka station is located as the brightest part of the picture. The diamond-shaped part of upper right was the ruins of

Fig.34
Central part of Shizuoka city was wrapped in flames in the early stage of air raid
(Possession of NARA/ Courtesy of Yozo Kudo)

V. 絵と写真が語る静岡の空襲
1. 6月20日 静岡空襲
(1) 2時間で燃え尽きた街

いきなり焼夷弾 (図39) が, 眠りについた人々を襲いました. 街を焼き, 人を焼いた炎の中を, 人々は夢中で逃げ惑いました. その記憶を残したいという人々が, 絵を描き, 手記を書いています. これらと写真から, 静岡の空襲をたどってみました.

6月20日未明, 第314航空団のB-29は, 伊豆半島波勝崎上空を通り, 海岸から市の中心部に侵入しました. 0時51分から2時54分にかけて, 123機のB-29から, 868トンの焼夷弾が投下され, 市街地の66%が焼き払われました (図42, 46).

空襲警報が鳴る間もなく, 駅周辺に焼夷弾が投下されました. 図34の航空写真は, 攻撃中の米軍機から撮影されたものです. 空襲が始まって間もなく, 市中心部はすでに炎に包まれています. 静岡駅は, フラッシュの下にあります. 右上の菱形部分は駿府城跡で, 静岡連隊が駐屯していました. この左外縁には県庁や市役所がありますが, 両方ともすでに炎に包まれています.

図34. 空襲が始まった頃, 静岡市中心部は炎に包まれている (米国立公文書館蔵／工藤洋三氏提供)

ここには，一瞬のうちに灼熱の地獄と化した街を，訳も分からず逃げ惑った，大勢の人々がいたのです．

次々と飛来するB-29は，街の至るところに，焼夷弾をまき散らしました．図35の絵は，図34の航空写真に写された地上の様子を，久保田光亭さんが描いたものです．外堀の向こうの市役所のドーム（左側）も，警察署の望楼も，みな火に包まれています．爆撃中心点は警察署の200m先に設定されていました．

市の中心部が燃えていく様を，安倍川に近い家から見ていた，当時18歳の杉本政裕さんは，以下のように記しています．[1]「父と壕の外へ出てみると，東北から南にかけて，城壁のようにそそり立つ大火炎と大黒煙．煙の先端は2000mを超すであろうか．その火炎の中から，B-29が機体を赤々と輝かせ，強風にあおられながら，爆撃体勢に入ってくる．爆撃高度は，非常に低い」

the Sunpu Castle, where the Shizuoka infantry regiment was stationed. Shizuoka prefectural office and the city hall are located in the left side of the diamond. Both buildings were in flames. Actually, there were a lot of people below the smoke, and they were desperately running about in the blazing inferno.

One after another, B-29s came and dropped incendiaries all over the urban area. Fig.35, drawn by Kotei Kubota, shows the scene at the very moment of the bombing as the aerial photograph (Fig.34). Everything, including the dome of city hall (left side) and the watchtower of police station on the other side of the moat, was wrapped in flames. Mean Point of Impact located 200 m away of the police station.

Masahiro Sugimoto, 18 years old at that time, who was watching the fire from his house near the Abe River, wrote that[1] "I went out of our air raid shelter with my father, and I watched the spreading fire and smoke walls as large as castle walls from north-east to south. The top of the smoke would be over 2,000 m. The B-29s brilliant bodies were fanned by the violent wind and looked ready to bomb. The bombing altitude was very low."

図35．市役所も警察署も炎に包まれた（久保田光亭画，当時45歳）

The city hall and the police station were in flames (Painted by Kotei Kubota, then age 45)

Fig.36 The smoke and fire spread in an instant around the Shizuoka station
(Possession of NARA / Courtesy of Yozo Kudo)

Fig.37 Run away in storm of flames
(Painted by Kiyo Serizawa, then age, 22)

(2) People ran away in the storm of flames

The aerial photograph of Fig.36 represented the burning Shizuoka station in flames. Kiyo Serizawa painted her experience in Fig.37.

Big fire generated strong ascending currents, which created whirlwinds everywhere. Sugiyama who lost two brothers in this fire wrote as follows:[4]

"The hot gust blew again. We were also blown away by a gust and returned back to the same place as where we had been. A woman was also blown off by a gust, and fell down right and left, screaming in terror. The incident repeated several times, and then she didn't move at all.

We missed two brothers whom we are supposed to be held by hand. Suddenly my mother burst into tears."

(2) 炎の嵐の中を

図36の航空写真は，静岡駅周辺部が，煙と炎に包まれている状況です．図37の絵は，地上のありさまを，芹沢きよさんが描いたものです．

大火災のために，激しい上昇気流が生じ，至るところに，つむじ風が発生しました．2人の弟を失った杉山さんの手記です．[4]

「…また熱い突風が吹く．私たちも吹き飛ばされ，いつの間にか元の場所に戻っていた．…目の前で女の人が突風に飛ばされ，大きな声を出しては右に倒れ，左に倒れ，それを何度も繰り返し，そのうち動かなくなった…．

母が手を引いて逃げた弟2人が見当たらない．母は急に泣き崩れた」

図36．またたく間に駅周辺に広がった煙と火災
（国立公文書館蔵／工藤洋三氏提供）

図37．荒れ狂う炎の嵐の中を逃げる
（芹沢きよ画，当時22歳）

焼夷弾に直撃された妹 (4)

矢部正昭さん (当時10歳) の手記より

家族で, 近所の防空壕へ逃げこんだ. 殺気立った空気を察したのか, 母に背負われた4歳の妹が, 火がついたように泣き出した. 近所の顔役から「うるさいから出て行け」と言われる. そのうち, ここにいては危険だと壕を出た. 辺りは逃げ惑う人で混乱していた. 私たちは焼夷弾の雨の下を, 賤機山(しずはたやま)の山裾に沿って, 北の妙見神社の方へ逃げる一群と共に走った.

そのうちにふと, 右腕に血の乾いたような妙な感触を感じて触ってみたが傷はない. このような緊急時にもかかわらず, 呑気にもこの不思議な状態を母に聞いてみたくなった.「お母さん, ぼくおかしいよ」と尋ねようと母の方を見た時, 私は言葉を飲み込んでしまった. 母の背には妹ではなくて, 赤黒い塊が乗っていたのだ.「恵がやられた!」と夢中で母に知らせた.「恵ではなく葵だよ」(図38). 母の絶叫は, 今も私の耳に残っている. 焼夷弾が母の肩に寄りかかっていた葵の頭を割り, 私は右半身に妹の血を浴びていたのだ. 母は, 頭を砕かれた娘を背負ったまま, 走り続けた.

火が迫り, トタンは熱風に舞い上がる. 上空を次々とB-29が飛んで行く. しばらく逃げた後, 布団の上に妹の死骸を横たえた. 三方から火が迫っている. どうせなら皆で死のうと, それ以上逃げるのを止めた…茶畑が火を食い止めてくれたおかげで, みんな助かった.

翌日, 炊き出しをもらうため学校へ行った私は, 同級生に優越感を感じていた.「俺の家は (お国の為) 犠牲者を出したんだぞ」と. 妹の死という代償を持つ優越感, 兄らしくない人間の心をなくした卑劣な心だ. 戦争は人の気持ちまでだめにしてしまう.

My younger sister was hit by incendiary bomb (4)

Masaaki Yabe, then age 10

When we evacuated into the air raid shelter nearby, my 4 years old sister who was on our mother's back, began to cry loudly under the menacing atmosphere. A community boss adjacent to us said, "Go out! You are so noisy." Soon, we felt so unwelcomed to stay in the shelter that we went out of the shelter. We saw the people who ran this way or that looking for a way out. We ran along the foot of Mt. Shizuhata, together with a group who ran toward the Myoken shrine.

Fig.38　Masaaki's sister, Aoi
図38. 正昭さんの妹, 葵ちゃん

Soon, I felt so peculiar like as my right arm was gone when I touched it. But, I wasn't injured. In spite of this kind of anxiety, I wanted to ask my mother about this strange experience. When I was going to see her to ask "Mom, I'm feeling strange.", I was lost with words. I couldn't see my sister on my mother's back but a mass of reddish black color. I cried to my mother with horror, "Kei is hit!" She told me, "Not Kei but Aoi" (Fig.38). Even now, I couldn't forget her scream at that time. The incendiary bomb hit my sister's head which was leaning over her mother's shoulder. So, the blood splashed on my right hand body, and that's why I felt strange. My mother kept running carrying her daughter's crushed body on her back.

The raging fire was approaching our place. Many galvanized iron sheets were blown up by the hot wind. One after another, B-29s flew over us. After while we ran away, my mother laid my sister's dead body on the cotton quilts. The fire approached us from three directions. We stopped running away because we thought that if we die, sooner or later, we want to die together. In reality, we survived because of the green tea plantation which stopped the fire from spreading.

Next day, I went to school to get rice balls given as voluntary food. I had a sense of pride for my sister's death as I explained to my classmates. "My family had a victim for the nation." It was a wrong feeling for humanity and brotherhood. The war also destroyed the mind of a human being.

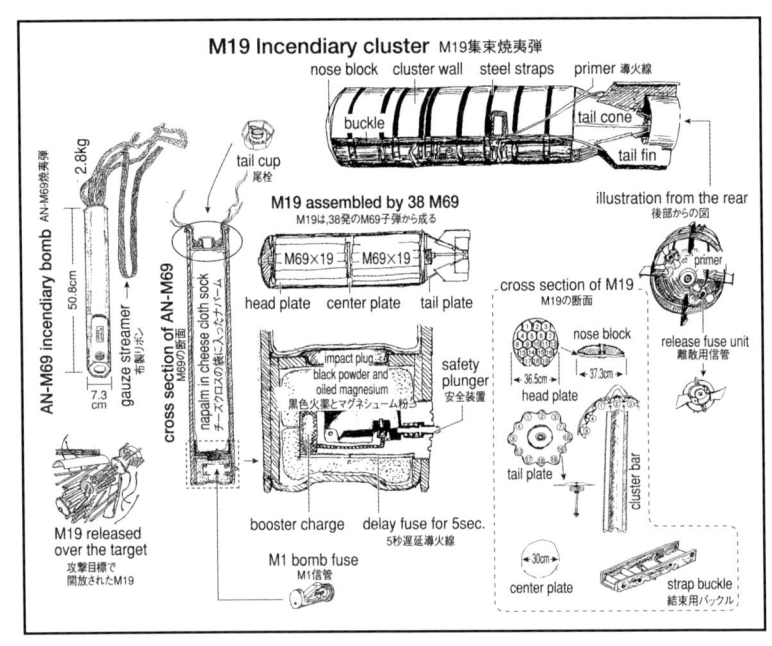

Fig.39 The structure of M19 (formerly called E46) Incendiary Cluster (after Eiichi Hoshi)
図39. M19（以前の呼称はE46）集束焼夷弾の構造（星栄一氏作図より）

Fig.40 A woman filled napalm into M69 pipe
(Possession of NARA/Courtesy of Yozo Kudo)
図40. ナパームをM69の筒に詰める女性
（米国立公文書館蔵／工藤洋三氏提供）

The Incendiary Bombs dropped on Shizuoka area

1) M19 (formerly called E46) 500 pounds incendiary cluster　　　　　Shizuoka city
2) M47 A2 100 pounds incendiary bomb　　　　　　　Shizuoka city & Shimizu city
3) M17 A1 500 pounds incendiary cluster　　　　　　　　　　　　　Shimizu city

1) Fig.39 shows the structure of M19 (formerly called E46) incendiary cluster. M19 was assembled by 38 bundles of M69. M69 was a steel hexagonal pipe with about 8 cm in diameter and about 50 cm in length, which was filled with napalm as shown in Fig.40. It was effective for creating fire. Therefore, M69 was mainly used on Japan for burning houses. The clusters were set to disperse around 1,000 m above the targets. A lot of M69 scattered and fell tied to four ribbons as a way to weaken the impact of the fall.

2) M47 was small sized napalm incendiary bomb of 31.8 kg with the ability of penetrating through roofs and caused huge fire explosion. The pathfinder mainly dropped them.

3) M17 consisted of 110 of M50 called magnesium-thermite incendiary. It generated high temperature and deep penetration. It was mainly used at the European front.

静岡地域に投下された焼夷弾

1) M19（以前の呼称はE46）500ポンド集束焼夷弾
2) M47A2 100ポンド焼夷弾
3) M17A1 500ポンド集束焼夷弾
静岡市には1)2)が，
清水市には2)3)が投下された．

1) 図39はM19（以前の呼称はE46）の構造図．M19はM69を38発集束している．M69は直径約8cm，長さ約50cmの鉄製の六角柱筒に，図40のようにナパームを詰めたもの．火災を発生させるため，主として日本家屋に多用された．集束弾は，目標の上空1000m前後で解束するように設定され，ばらばらになったM69は，4本のリボンを引いて落下した．リボンは落下の衝撃を抑え，延焼効果を高めた．

2) M47は31.8kgの小型ナパーム爆弾．貫通力が大きいので，屋根を突き抜け，大火災と共に爆発を起こす．先導機が主に投下した．

3) M17はM69より小型のM50を110本集束．マグネシウム・テルミット焼夷弾とも呼ばれ，高温を発し大きな貫通力を持つ．欧州で多用された．

(3) 安倍川へ

四方を火で囲まれた人々は，少しでも暗い方へ，または安倍川を目指して逃げました．

安倍川橋のたもとにある，安倍川餅の石部屋の娘さんは，それを見てこう記しています．[4]

「家の前の道路は，市街から逃げてきた人でごったがえし，自転車，荷車，乳母車，叫び声，泣き声，怒声が黒い山となって，安倍川橋をめがけていた…．土手の大楠木から見る静岡市は，端から端まで火の海，家も学校も火柱となって，焼け落ちた．翌日から隣の空き地には，市内から焼死体が運ばれ，一列に丸太のように並べられた．死体は日に日に増し，隅から一体ずつ河原で荼毘にふされた…」

1分間に1機の割合で飛来し，市の中心部に焼夷弾を落とした123機のB-29は，左旋回して安倍川を渡り，基地へ帰りました（図42）．図41はその様子を安倍川の土手から眺めていた当時8歳の滝さんが描いた絵です．遠くから見ていた人々は，「まるで花火のようだった」と言います．

図41．集束弾の束がはずれ，バラバラになって夜空を落ちて来る焼夷弾
（滝正臣画，当時8歳）

Fig.41 Incendiary Clusters were released and scattered in the dark sky
(Painted by Masaomi Taki, then age 8)

(3) Heading the Abe River

Surrounded by flames in all directions, people ran away toward hiding areas or the Abe River. A daughter of Sekibeya, the owner of a famous traditional confectionary shop near the Abe River, wrote as follows:[4]

"The road in front of my house was filled by people who ran away from the town. The sound of bicycle, handcart, baby-car, cry, howl and roar were all mixed up and formed a massive black mountain, which headed toward the Abe River. I watched the city area under a big camphor tree on the bank of the Abe River. Shizuoka, from end to end, was just a sea of flame. Lots of houses and buildings, including my school, became pillars of fire and were burnt down. Many charred bodies were gathered at the neighboring vacant lot, and put in a row like logs from the following day. Dead bodies found in the ruins from fire increased day by day, and cremated one by one in order on the dry riverbed of the Abe River."

123 B-29s flew over Shizuoka every minute, and made a turn to the left (Fig.42). Fig.41 was drawn by Masaomi Taki who watched the bombing scene from the bank of the Abe River. Many people watching the bombings from a distance said, "It looked just like fireworks."

Young men caught B-29s bombing Shizuoka
−They recorded about B-29s at the Fujieda and Kambara observation post−

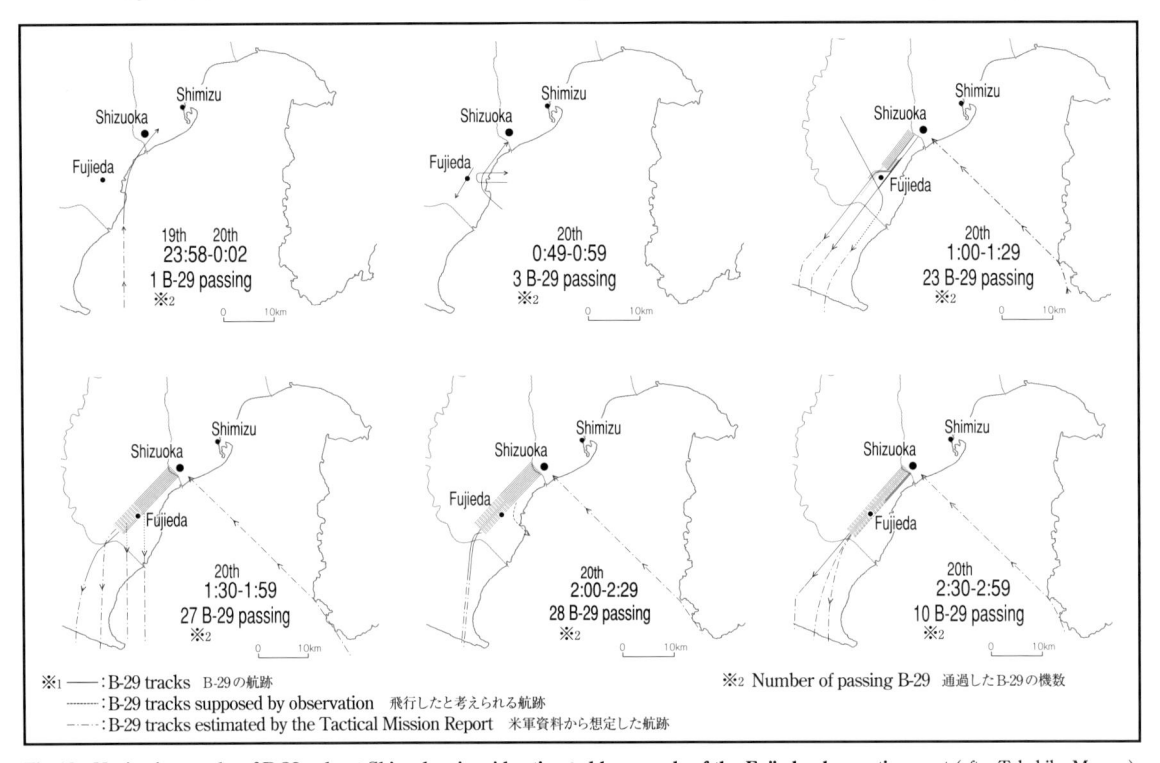

Fig.42 Navigation tracks of B-29s about Shizuoka air raid estimated by records of the Fujieda observation post (after Takahiko Murase)
図42. 藤枝防空監視哨の記録から推定される静岡空襲時のB-29の航跡（村瀬隆彦氏作成より）

Fig.42 was drawn based on the historical document recorded at the Fujieda observation post, by Takahiko Murase.[4]

It is shown that an airplane approached from Omaezaki before midnight of June 20 was presumed a weather air plane.

And this figure shows that the full-scale air raid began after 1:00 a.m., July 20. Each B-29 approached from Hagachizaki, Izu peninsula, continued to bomb till about 3:00 a.m.

These facts support the description of the Tactical Mission Report by the XXI Bomber Command.

静岡空襲のB-29を捉えた青年たち
− 藤枝と蒲原の防空監視哨で，B-29の動きを記録していた −

図42は藤枝防空監視哨の記録を基に，村瀬隆彦さんが作成したもの.[4]

図中，20日になる前に，御前崎から侵入した1機が観測されますが，これは風程観測機と思われます.

伊豆半島波勝崎から，B-29は1機ずつ飛来し，本格的な空襲は20日1時頃から始まり3時頃まで続けられました.

これらは，第21爆撃機集団による作戦任務報告書の記述を裏付けています.

(4) 一夜明けて
　　「私，生きていた…」

「爆音が遠のいて…東の空が白み始める…空の下半分が雲海のようで，その中から見たこともないくらい大きな黒くすすけた太陽が，ゆらめきながら昇ってきたの…しばし呆然…我に返って，ああ生きていたんだ」と思ったと，町塚みよさん．[4]

つい数時間前まで，家族の団欒を育んでいた家々も，学校も，商店街も，生活の場は焼け落ちて瓦礫となり，焼け死んだ人々は物体となりました．

生き残った人々は，行方不明になった肉親を求めて，黒こげの死体を飛び越えながら，焼けトタンの一枚一枚をめくって歩きました．また大通りの両脇に，ぎっしり並べられた死体を，一つ一つ見て回りました．図46は静岡市の被災図です．

当時14歳の龍彦少年はその衝撃を，鎮魂の思いを込めて図43に描き，記しています．[2]

「一番町方面の広い通りに，焼けトタンをかぶせられた真っ黒こげの死体を見た．晴天なのに，くすぶり続ける熱気のためか，あたりは黄色くけぶっていた」

図43．路上に，焼けトタンをかぶせられた黒こげの死体があった
（遠藤龍彦画，当時14歳）

(4) The day after "I am alive"

"B-29's roar went away, the eastern sky was getting light, and the lower half of the sky looked like a sea of clouds, then a darkened big sun by smut, which we've never seen, was rising slowly. I was stupefied for a while, I came to myself, and realized that I was alive." Miyo Machizuka said.[4]

Many houses where people were having a good time only a few hours before, a lot of schools and shopping streets were changed to debris, and people burnt to death became "objects".

People who survived looked around a devastated field, stepped over the charred bodies, and looked for missing relatives under each galvanized iron sheet. Some people looked at each dead in rows on both sides of the big streets. Fig.46 shows disaster figure.

A boy named Tatsuhiko, 14 years old, painted Fig.43 and wrote that shocking scene for a requiem as follows:[2]

"I looked at scorched black dead bodies covered by burned galvanized iron sheets, in the wide street near Ichibancho. The air was yellowish smoky in spite of fine weather."

Fig.43　There were scorched black corpses covered in galvanized iron sheets
(Painted by Tatsuhiko Endo, then age 14)

A young girl and her little brother crushed by B-29

At about 2:30 a.m., when Shizuoka city was burning fiercely, two B-29s collided in air and both crashed into the banks of the Abe River.

The tail of one aircraft fell into the mulberry field. Two young men and two little Japanese children died.

Chieko Sawamoto, 14 years old, was wandering around the embankment. She wrote as follows: [1]

"At that time, I watched a crying young mother who was holding her two dead little children. They were a family of the soy cake (*Tofu*) store, where I'd been. Although I was only 14 years old at that time, I experienced too many incidents in such a short time. Now, as a mother, I can share pains of three mothers, one lost two little children, and the other two lost their sons in the B-29 crash that night."

Isao Arai who evacuated from Tokyo to Shizuoka and lived near the soy cake store in his childhood, had been trying to find the information on his two friends (Fig.44) for a long time. He couldn't forget the conversation with them "See you tomorrow!" when they parted for home that evening. Several hours later, B-29s attacked Shizuoka.

62 years since then, he could meet their 1 year old sister who ran away on her mother's back, at last. Their mother already died. Their sister, Yoko didn't know what happened that night. Then, Yoko said,

"I was not interested in the war, but now I realized that the day of the Shizuoka Air Raid, June 20, is deeply related to me."

Fig.44 Left: Masae Takasu, then age 10
Right: Yoshiharu Takasu, then age 8
(Courtesy of Yoko Takasu)

B-29の下敷きになった幼い姉弟

市内一帯が燃え盛っていた午前2時半頃, 2機のB-29が衝突し安倍川の両岸に墜落しました.

1機の尾翼部分は, 川岸にある桑畑に落ち, 2人の若いアメリカ兵が墜落死しました. そして, 2人の幼い子どもの命が奪われました.

土手をさまよっていた当時14才の沢本千恵子さんは,

「その時, B-29に当たって死んだ2人の幼い姉弟に, しがみついて号泣する, 若い母親の姿が目に入りました. 私も買いに行ったことのある, お豆腐屋さんの人たちでした. …14歳の私は, 短い時間に, あまりにも多くのできごとを体験しました. …母親になった今, あの夜, 2人の幼い子どもを失った母親の気持ち, そしてたとえ敵であっても, 異国の地で果てた若者たち, その2人の母親の気持ちが, 痛みとして返ってきます」と記しています. [1]

子どもの頃, 東京から豆腐屋さんの近所に疎開していた新井勲さんは, 長年, この姉弟 (図44) の消息を捜していました. 夕方, 家に帰り際に「また明日遊ぼうね!」と言って別れたことが忘れられませんでした. この数時間後に, 静岡はB-29に襲われたのです.

新井さんは62年後, ついにあの夜, 母親に背負われて逃げた, 当時1歳の妹さんに会うことができました. すでに母親は他界, 妹の陽子さんは, この事実を知らされずに育ちました. そして, 「これまで戦争は他人事でしたが, 真実を知った今, 静岡空襲の日, 6月20日は, 私の原点です」と語っています.

図44.
左:姉の高須雅枝さん (当時10歳)
右:弟の高須義治さん (当時8歳)
(高須陽子さん提供)

火葬場となった安倍川の河原

焼け跡の死体処理には, 静岡連隊の兵隊, 囚人などが当たりました. 死亡者の数は, 火葬場の処理能力をはるかに超えたため, 市は安倍川の河原で死体を荼毘にふしました.

空襲の数日後, 安倍川橋を訪れた当時中等学校3年生の小川孝太郎さんは, 河原で青い服の囚人たちが死体を運んでいる光景を目にし, 図45の絵と, 以下の手記を残しています.[2]

「こげた死体の黒, 死体を焼く煙の白, 受刑者たちの制服の青, この3つの色は, 今もなお私の目に深く焼きついてはなれない.」

身内の遺体を, 家族の手で火葬した人々も多数いました. 他人の遺骨と混じってしまう恐れもあったからです. 斉藤静枝さんは, お母さんと妹2人を失い, お父さんと共に, 火葬しました.[2]

「親の死体を子どもが焼くという, この地獄のような恐ろしいことも, ああ言ったり, こう言ったり, 悲しんでいるいとまはなかった. 周りは, 死体を焼く異様な臭いに満ちていた. 父は, ひと言も言わなかった. 感情のなくなった人のように, 黙々と木切れを燃やし続けた. それはちょうど, 網で魚を焼く時と, 同じようだった…」

図45. 死体は安倍川の河原で火葬された (小川孝太郎画, 当時15歳)

Fig.45 The corpse was cremated at the riverbed of the Abe River
(Painted by Kotaro Ogawa , then age 15)

The dry riverbed of the Abe River as crematory

Many soldiers of Shizuoka infantry regiment and prisoners collected the corpses and cremated them. The number of dead people was more than the capacity of the crematory could hold that the municipality decided to cremate them at the dry riverbed of the Abe River.

A few days later, Kotaro Ogawa who was the third year student of junior high school, went to the bridge of the Abe River and watched some prisoners in blue uniform carried the dead bodies. He painted Fig.45 and wrote as follows:[2]

"Black was the color of charred corpse, white was the color of smoke burning corpses, and blue was the prisoner's uniform color, I'll never forget these three colors."

There were many people who cremated their families and relatives on their own. They were afraid of mixing family's ashes of others. Shizue Saito lost her mother and 2 sisters. She and her father cremated them. She wrote as follows:[2]

"Although I conducted an awful infernal act – burning my mother's dead body as a child – I had no time to lament or say anything. The burning corpse's odd smell filled the air. My father said nothing. He kept adding wood to the fire silently as if he had lost all feelings. It was just like burning fish on a grill."

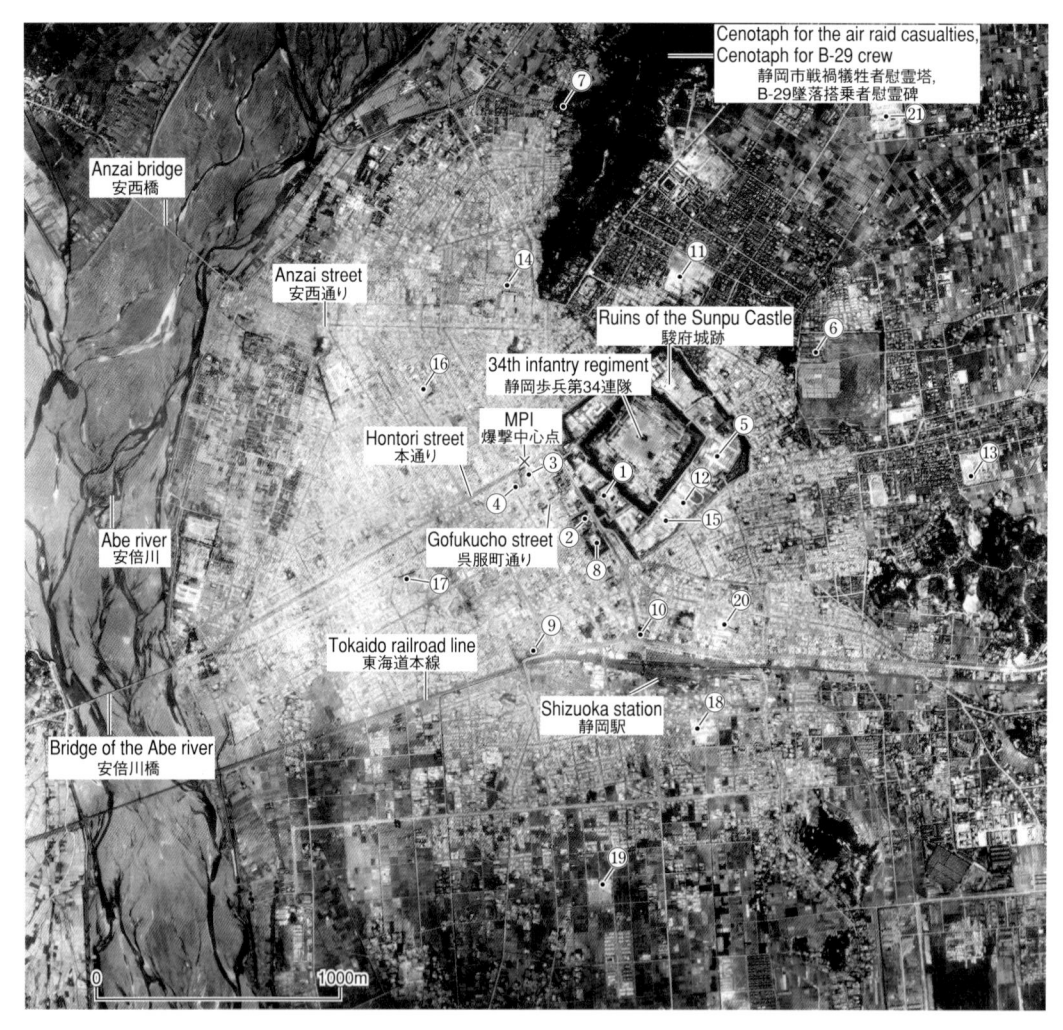

Fig.46 The disaster figure of Shizuoka city The Mitsubishi and Sumitomo works in the south part of the city located beyond the scope of the map. Numbered points in the map are shown as follows.

図46. 静岡市の被災図 静岡市の南部にある三菱工場と住友工場は，この図の範囲外になっている．図中の番号は，以下の施設に対応する

1	Shizuoka prefectural office　静岡県庁	12	Normal school　静岡師範学校男子部
2	Shizuoka city hall　静岡市役所	13	Women's normal school　静岡師範学校女子部
3	Bank of Shizuoka　静岡銀行	14	Anzai national elementary school　安西国民学校
4	Fukyoraian　不去来庵	15	Attached national elementary school　静岡師範学校付属国民学校
5	Shizuoka prison　静岡刑務所	16	Ichibancho national elementary shool　一番町国民学校
6	Military drill ground　練兵場	17	Shintori national elementary school　新通国民学校
7	Myoken shrine　妙見神社	18	Morishita national elementary school　森下国民学校
8	Goyotei, cottage for the emperor　御用邸	19	Nakada national elementary school　中田国民学校
9	Hodai temple for the Tokugawa　宝台院	20	Tenmacho national elementary school　伝馬町国民学校
10	Matsuzakaya department store　松坂屋百貨店	21	Shizuoka girls junior high school　静岡高等女学校
11	Shizuoka junior high school　静岡中学校		

2. 7月7日　清水空襲

静岡空襲の夜空をこがす炎を見, また通勤・通学の途中で, 静岡の惨状を見て来た人たちは, その凄まじさに戦慄し, 「次は清水だ」と実感しました. そしてついに, その日, 7月7日はやって来ました.

逃げようとしていた人々も, 想像以上の速さで降ってくる焼夷弾の恐ろしさに半ば呆然とし, 火の海に囲まれて逃げ遅れました. 風間照江さん (17歳) は,

「火に追われて, 港橋近くの巴川に入った. 橋の下は焼夷弾を避けようと, 人がいっぱいで入れない. なんとか川の中で, 首だけ出していた. 2時間くらいして水かさが増え, 背が立たなくなった. 20人以上が, 流されて溺死したという」と記しています.[5]
図47の絵は, 風間さんの体験を聞き, 鈴木玲之さんが描いたものです.

米軍資料によると, 第313航空団のB-29は, 駿河湾を横切って, 東から清水に侵入しました. 第6回目の中小都市空襲でした. そのうち133機が, 7日0時33分から2時10分にかけて, M47焼夷爆弾と, M17集束焼夷弾を投下. 街の約50%を破壊しました.

図47. 港橋の下に逃げて
(鈴木玲之画, 当時17歳／風間照江の体験, 当時17歳)

2. July 7th　Shimizu Air Raid

Some people in Shimizu watched the raging flames of Shizuoka air raid and the others watched the terrible scenes on their way to school or to office. Therefore, they supposed, with fear, that B-29s next target would be Shimizu. At last, the day, July 7 came.

Many people, running away from fire, failed to escape the incendiary bombs that dropped faster than they could have imagined. They were wrapped in fire. Terue Kazama, 17 years old, wrote as follows:[5]

"Blazing fire made us enter the Tomoe River near the Minato Bridge. We tried to hide under this bridge, but the place was already filled with people and no space left for me. We went into the river while keeping our heads above water. But after 2 hours, we could no longer stand in it because of the rising water. I heard more than 20 people were driven away and died." Fig.47 was drawn by Reiji Suzuki after he heard the experience of Terue.

According to the U.S. Army documents, the 313 Wing flew over the Suruga Bay from the east and headed toward Shimizu. It was the sixth attack on the small cities. 133 B-29s dropped M47 incendiary bomb and M17 incendiary cluster from 0:33 a.m. to 2:10 a.m., and destroyed 50% of the built-up area of Shimizu city.

Fig.47　Taking refuge under the Minato bridge
(Painting by Reiji Suzuki, story by Terue Kazama, when they were 17 years old)

Crossing a bridge over the Tomoe River, Reiji Suzuki and his family barely escaped from town, he painted Fig.48 and wrote.[5]

"Incendiary bombs were dropped again while we were running on a slope in front of a church. When the sound of dropping incendiary, like heavy rain falls stopped, I looked up to the sky and saw the huge body of a B-29 flying over our heads. I could see a pilot. A boy wrapped in flames ran away crying like a madman on my right side. Later, I heard he died at that slope." The day after, the eastern sky in glowing light from the blazing inferno that made the urban area into a sea of flame was finally over. The central part of Shimizu city was completely devastated. But we couldn't go back home because of the high temperature and the hot whirlwind.

The gross weight of M47 incendiary bomb and M19 incendiary cluster dropped on Shizuoka was 868 tons, and on Shimizu 1030 tons. Although the urban area of Shimizu was about 40% of Shizuoka area, incendiary bombs dropped over Shimizu were far more than those in Shizuoka in ratio. But the damage of Shimizu was relatively small – 50% of the built-up area and the number of the dead was 151. These unexpected results could probably be explained from the facts that people in Shimizu ran away once the bombings started, and houses were sparsely spread from north to the south along the coast.

Fig.48　A requiem for a boy　A boy wrapped in flames ran away crying like a madman (Painted by Reiji Suzuki)

焼夷弾の雨の中, 家族と共にやっとの思いで橋を渡って逃げて来た鈴木玲之さんは, 手記と共に, 図48の絵を描きました.[5]

「…カトリック教会の坂にさしかかると, 再び焼夷弾の雨. ザーという焼夷弾の投下音が鳴り止み, 助かったと, 突っ伏していた顔を上げると, 今しもB-29の巨体が頭上を通りすぎるところだった. パイロットの姿が見えた. 私の右側を, 一人の少年が火達磨になり, 泣き叫びながら狂ったように走って行く. 後でこの坂の上で死んだと聞いた」

夜が明けて, 空が明るみ始めた頃, 市街を火の海にした劫火(ごうか)は消え, 中心部は焼け野原になりました. しかし, 未だに高温で, 熱風がつむじ風となって吹き荒れ, すぐには焼跡に戻ることはできませんでした.

静岡に投下された焼夷弾は, M47とM19を合わせて868トン. 対して清水は1030トンでした. 静岡の40%の狭い面積に, 多量の焼夷弾が投下されたことになります. しかし, 清水の面積焼夷率は50%, 死亡者は151人と, 被害が小さかった理由は, 人々は空襲が始まるとすぐ逃げたこと, 住宅は海岸に沿って南北にまばらに広がり, 密集していなかったことが挙げられます.

図48. 少年への鎮魂　炎に包まれた少年が, 狂ったように叫びながら走って行った(鈴木玲之画)

3. 7月31日　艦砲射撃

清水空襲から1カ月もたたない7月31日の0時過ぎ、今度は海からの砲弾が、清水市内の清水町などを襲いました。

突然、激しい爆発音が響きわたり、砲弾が人々を直撃、44人が亡くなりました。

米軍資料は、午前0時5分から9分にかけて、7隻の駆逐艦が砲撃したと記録していますが、長い間、清水の人々は潜水艦からの砲撃と信じていました。

しかし、1998年、アメリカ・オレゴン州のロナルド・ソーシーさんから、「清水ふだん着の国際交流会」へ一通の手紙が届きました。彼は19歳の時、清水を攻撃した駆逐艦の乗組員だったのです（図49）。定年後、彼は、ずっと気になっていた清水への爆撃を、米国立公文書館で調べました。当夜の砲撃は、駿河湾に侵入した、第25駆逐艦隊の駆逐艦7隻によることを知り、清水の人々に知らせてくれたのです。その後、彼は清水を訪問し、友情を育みました。

この作戦は米海軍によるもので、7月から8月にかけて、第3艦隊第38機動部隊がフィリピンから日本近海に出動、北は室蘭から南は呉までの製鉄所や飛行場、造船所などが激しい攻撃を受けました。

幼い日の体験とソーシーさんの助言を基に、渡邉晴朗さんは、日本の資料や米軍資料を調べ、攻撃の詳細を明らかにしました。

図49．左は若き日のソーシーさん
（望月美貴子さん提供）

3. July 31st　Ship's Bombardment

Within a month from Shimizu air raid, shortly after midnight of July 31, Shimizu-cho and other places in Shimizu were attacked by the naval vessels off the coast.

Suddenly, heavy explosion echoed through the midnight sky. The bombs dropped on many houses and people, and 44 persons died.

Fig.49　Left is Ronald Soucy in his young days
(Courtesy of Kimiko Mochizuki)

The U.S. military documents recorded that 7 destroyers blasted from 0:05 a.m. to 0:09 a.m., but many people in Shimizu have believed that they were hit by submarines for a long time.

In 1998, "the Shimizu International Friendship Association" received a letter from Ronald Soucy, Oregon, U.S.A. He was 19 years old when he was one of the crew members of the destroyer that attacked Shimizu (Fig.49). After retirement, he studied the bombardment against Shimizu at the National Archives and Records Administration. He'd kept that incident in mind and never forgot. He knew that the bombardment was carried out by 7 destroyers of ComDesRon 25 that sailed into the Suruga Bay, and reported these facts to people in Shimizu. After that, he visited Shimizu city and extended friendship to the Japanese people.

This mission was carried out by the Navy, July through August. THIRD Fleet Task Force 38 proceeded towards the Japanese homelands from the Philippines. An iron work, aircraft industry, shipyards and so on, from Muroran in the north to Kure in the south were severely bombarded.

Based on his youth's experience of the bombardment and Soucy's advice, Haruo Watanabe studied the documents of Japan and the U.S. military documents, and explained the bombardment of that night in detail.

4. August 1st-2nd Final air raid on shimizu
Aftermath of Congratulatory big bombardment for Air Force Day

The Kageyama family who lost their house, the air raid on July 7, stayed with their relatives at Yamato-cho. After 9:00 p.m., on August 1, houses were suddenly struck. Many people nearby were buried alive under the debris. 32 persons were killed. Many people in that area experienced bombardments three times — July 7, July 31, and August 1. After midnight on August 2, the factories and warehouses in Mihokaijima, Hinode-cho were attacked by incendiary bombs.

On the same day that Shimizu was under attack, Hachioji, Toyama, Nagaoka and Mito were attacked at night with incendiaries that became the thirteenth attacks on small cities. Kawasaki Petroleum Complex was attacked by high-explosive bombs at night. Shimizu was included in the air raids. The operation on the 4 cities was the largest attack ever as 858 B-29s joined together and 5,128 tons of incendiaries were dropped. Each city was devastated 65% to 99%. The reasons for such heavy air raids on August 1 were recently clarified. The reason was that it was a memorial event of the U.S. Army Air Force Day.

From July through August, they operated the Psychological Leaflet Warfare which dropped many warning leaflets (Fig.50) over the targets and assigned cities were bombed soon afterwards. 16 cities including above cities out of 32 warned cities were actually attacked.

Fig.50 4 cities were attacked after dropping this leaflet (Courtesy of Yozo Kudo)

---

4. 8月1-2日 最後の清水空襲
米陸軍航空軍創設記念
大祝賀爆撃の余波

7月7日の空襲で、焼け出された影山さん一家は、大和町の親戚の家に身を寄せていました。8月1日21時過ぎ、突然、家もろとも吹き飛ばされ、大勢の人が瓦礫の中に埋もれました。32人が死亡。この地域の人々にとっては、7日、31日に続き、3度目の空襲でした。さらに2日の0時過ぎ、日の出町と三保貝島に焼夷弾が落ち、工場や倉庫が燃えました。

同日、八王子・富山・長岡・水戸が第13回中小都市空襲を受け、川崎石油コンビナートが爆撃されました。清水の空襲は、川崎と八王子を爆撃したB-29の余波でした。この中小都市空襲は過去最大、858機のB-29が出撃、4都市に5128トンの焼夷弾を投下。各都市は街の65%から99%を焼失しました。

なぜこの日、これほど大規模な空襲が行われたのか、長い間、謎でしたが、その理由が解けました。この日の攻撃は、米陸軍航空軍創設記念日の祝賀大爆撃だったのです。

米軍はまた、7月から8月にかけて、図50のような攻撃予告のリーフレットを撒き、その後直ちに空襲する、というリーフレット心理作戦を展開しました。32都市が予告され、上記の都市を含む16都市が攻撃されています。

図50. リーフレット投下後、4都市が空襲された (工藤洋三氏提供)

5. 空襲は続く…
パンプキンが島田を襲った

空前の被害を受けた8月1日の空襲以降も、空襲は続けられました.

そしてついに、8月6日、人類史上初の原爆が広島に投下され、3日後には、2つ目の原爆が長崎に投下されました. 街は一瞬にして廃墟と化し、大勢の人々の命が奪われ、いまだ多くの人々が、放射線の後遺症に苦しみ、心に深い傷を抱えています.

近年、原爆と同一の弾道を持ち、同重量5トンの訓練用模擬原爆、通称「パンプキン」が49発、日本各地に投下されたことが明らかになりました. この作戦は原爆投下部隊である第509混成群団によって、7月20日から8月14日にかけて挙行され、400人を超える人々の命を奪いました.

静岡県でも7月26日、島田、焼津、浜松にパンプキンが投下されました. 悪天候のため、富山市の工業地域を爆撃できなかった第509混成群団が、目標を変えて、前述の3地域を爆撃したのでした.

島田市扇町に投下された、1発のパンプキンは、多数の家屋を吹き飛ばしました（図51）. 即死者35人、重傷死者15人、負傷者150余人.

図51. 普門院のイチョウの上半分が吹き飛ばされた（米国立公文書館蔵／工藤洋三氏提供）

5. Bombing continued
Pumpkin attacked a lot of people at Shimada

Even after the attack on August 1-2 which gave the most devastating damages, air raids continued.

Finally, on August 6, the first atomic bomb was dropped on human beings and exploded over Hiroshima, and three days later a second atomic bomb was dropped on Nagasaki. Both cities were destroyed in a moment, and so many people were killed and injured. A lot of survivors are still suffering from the aftereffects of the atomic radiation and the trauma of terrible experiences.

Recently, the facts emerged revealing 49 practice bombs so called "Pumpkin bomb" as the same shape of 5 tons and ballistic character as the real atomic bomb were dropped in many places in Japan. This missions using Pumpkin were operated from July 20 through August 14 by the 509th Composite Group, organized to drop the atomic bomb. More than 400 people were killed by the Pumpkin.

In Shizuoka prefecture, Shimada, Yaizu and Hamamatsu were bombed by pumpkins on July 26. In reality, the 509th Composite Group was ordered to drop the Pumpkins on the industrial area in Toyama city, but they could not drop the bombs because of the bad weather. Therefore they changed the targets and dropped the Pumpkins on above-mentioned three areas.

One Pumpkin was dropped on Ogi-machi, Shimada city, that blew many houses away (Fig.51) and injured lots of residents: instant death – 35: severely wounded and death –15: injury – more over 150.

Fig.51 The upper half of a gingko in Fumon Temple was blown away by a Pumpkin bomb
(Possession of NARA / Courtesy of Yozo Kudo)

6. From the Ruined towns

Fig.52 Shimizu city in the following day of the air raid
(Photographed by Toshihiko Yamanashi)

図52.　清水空襲翌日の清水市内
(山梨年彦氏撮影)

Fig.53 The shanties and patches in the field of ash after the Shizuoka air raid
(Photographed by Ryuhei Yamanashi)

図53.　静岡空襲後，市内の焼け跡に建つバラックと畑 (山梨龍平氏撮影)

The incendiary attacks on the small urban areas continued until August 15 — the day the war ended.

After the war, all that remained were ruins all over town (Fig.52). People collected tinplates and wood remains and built the shanties. They cultivated the field of ash and restarted their lives (Fig.53).

6. 廃墟の街から

　中小都市に対する夜間焼夷空襲は、8月15日まで続けられました。

　そしてその日、戦争は終わりました。後に残ったのは、見渡す限りの廃墟でした (図52)。しかし人々は、焼けトタンや焼けた木っ端を拾い集め、バラックを建て、畑を作り、再生への道を歩み始めました (図53)。

Fig.54　Storehouse remained in Shizuoka
(Photographed by CIC/ Possession of NARA/ Courtesy of Yozo Kudo)

図54.　静岡市内の焼け残った土蔵（米民間情報部撮影／米国立公文書館蔵／工藤洋三氏提供）

Fig.55　A boy carrying a baby on his back on Route 1　(Photographed by CIC/Possession of NARA/Courtesy of Yozo Kudo)

図55.　国道1号線で子守をする少年（米民間情報部撮影／米国立公文書館蔵／工藤洋三氏提供）

　日本は戦後，GHQの統治下に置かれました．図54, 55は米民間情報部が撮影した写真です．図55は，静岡市郊外，丸子地区の終戦後の風景．英語の交通標識のそばで，笑顔の少年が，赤ん坊を背負い子守をしています．

　子どもに，笑みが戻ってきました．

After the war, Japan was under the rule of General Headquarters. Figs.54 and 55 were photographed by the Counter Intelligence Corps. Fig.55 shows a postwar scene in Mariko area located in the suburbs of Shizuoka. A laughing boy carried a baby on his back near the English traffic signs.

　Smiles came back to children.

7. The Cenotaphs

Fig.56 Fukumatsu Ito built the Cenotaph for the crashed B-29 crew

図56.　伊藤福松さんは，墜落したB-29搭乗員のための墓碑を建てた

Fig.57 The cenptaphs for the aira raid victims (right) and the crashed B-29 crew (left) at the summit of Mt.Shizuhata

図57.　賤機山山頂に建つ静岡市戦禍犠牲者慰霊塔（右）と，B-29墜落搭乗者慰霊碑（左）

One B-29 crashed into the courtyard of the fish dealer "Uocho" near the bank of Abe River. Fukumatsu Ito, one of the relatives of "Uocho", said "There was no difference between friend and foe after death", and built the cenotaph for the crashed B-29's crew (Fig.56).

He and his supporters built two cenotaphs, one is for the victims of the Shizuoka air raid, and the other for the crashed B-29's crew at the summit of the Mt. Shizuhata, in 1970 (Fig.57, 46). A joint memorial service has been carried out by the volunteers of Shizuoka and the officer of U.S. Army from the Yokota base since 1977.

Now, this mountain is a good hiking path where we can look down across the Shizuoka city with Mt. Fuji in the background.

7. 慰霊

　B-29の1機は安倍川の土手に近い魚屋「魚長」の中庭に落ちました．親戚の一人，伊藤福松さんは「死んでしまえば，敵も味方もない」．こう言って，墜落死したB-29搭乗員のための慰霊碑を建てました（図56）．

　その後1970年，有志と共に賤機山の山頂に，空襲犠牲者と，B-29搭乗員の慰霊碑を建てました（図57, 46）．1977年からは，横田基地の米軍も参加し，毎年，日米合同慰霊祭が続けられています．

　賤機山は現在，ハイキングコースになっており，頂上からは，富士山を背景にした静岡市を，一望の下に見渡すことができます．

The sight of my town from the Mt. Shizuhata 65 years ago would be a sea of fire. Wars insult human beings, destroy culture, harm the natural environment, and injure the earth. Wars are started by human beings, so I believe that human beings can also stop wars.

　65年前，賤機山の山頂から見た街は，炎のるつぼだったことでしょう．戦争は，人間を貶め，培ってきた文化を瓦礫とし，自然を根こそぎ破壊し，そして地球を痛めます．戦争は人間がつくるもの，つくらないこともできるはずです．

Acknowledgement

When I visited Miya Kameyama, who lost 5 relatives in an air raid, she said to me "I couldn't die till I let people know that painful incident." The outline of the Shizuoka air raid including the mission's purpose which resulted in Kameyama family's death has been revealed from the US Army archives and the Japanese historical materials. We published "The documentary of the Shizuoka & Shimizu Air Raid" in 2005, and handed it to Miya. She was pleased and relieved. Miya died in 2008 at 97 years old, imagine that Miya reported this to her relatives in Heaven.

Would it console the surviving family if the realities of air raid were made public? I have had this question for a long time. But I felt relieved when I saw MIya's comforted face.

The English Version of the Shizuoka Air Raid is finally out. This book is based on "The Documentary of the Shizuoka & Shimizu Air Raid", supported by a lot of people as follows. I especially gratefully acknowledge Mr. Yozo Kudo for the help on English translation, his valuable advices and information, and Ms. Diana Lee for help on proofreading. Also I would like to thank Mr. Cary Karacas, City University New York, for his kind encouragement. I am grateful to "Shizuoka Peace Center" for many materials which became the basis of this book. Ms. Sumiko Konagaya and the late Mr. Reiji Suzuki always encouraged me. Mr. Takahiko Murase gave me the proper advice related to history. The late Ms. Chisako Sakurai, Ms. Akiko Kusano, Ms. Kazuko Isaji, Ms. Shizuko Shiotsu, Ms. Michiko Ishigami, Ms. Masako Kusano and Ms. Ryoko Sato supported both physically and spiritually. I am thankful to them all. Also I would like to thank the Sumida City Museum, the Yamanashi photographic studio, Mr. Isao Hino and many other people who supported me.

I lost two intimate friends – Ms. Chisako Sakurai and Mr. Reiji Suzuki – who had the same intention with me, but passed away before this book comes out. Chisako cheered me from Heaven, and Reiji gave me advice under medical treatment. Such encouragement became a big motivation. I would like to dedicate this book to all the war victims, the late Ms. Chisako and the late Mr. Reiji.

謝 辞

かつて空襲の聞き取り調査で，亀山みやさんをお訪ねしたことがありました．5人のご親類を失ったみやさんは，「このことを皆に知らせなければ，死ぬに死ねない」と語られました．米軍資料や日本の資料などの調査から，空襲の作戦意図を含む全体像が明らかになり，2005年に「静岡・清水空襲の記録」を出版しました．亀山さんにお届けすると，安堵の表情を浮かべ，喜んでくださいました．昨年，亀山さんは97歳で亡くなられましたが，天国で皆様に報告されていると思います．

空襲の実態を明らかにするのは，ご遺族にとって慰めの一端となるのでしょうか．このことをずっと考えてきましたが，亀山さんの晴れやかなお顔に救われた思いがしました．

ようやく念願の英語版ができました．この本は「静岡・清水空襲の記録」を基にしていますが，今回も大勢の人々に支えられて完成しました．中でも，英訳では工藤洋三さんに終始多大なご協力をいただき，また内容へのご助言や資料提供をいただきました．また Diana Lee さんに，英訳の校正をしていただきました．厚く御礼申し上げます．NY市立大の Cary Karacas さんの励ましにも深く感謝します．静岡平和資料センターからは，多くの資料を提供していただきました．小長谷澄子さん，故鈴木玲之さんには，常に温かい励ましをいただきました．村瀬隆彦さんに歴史の章でご助言をいただき，故桜井知佐子さん，草野明子さん，伊佐治和子さん，塩津慎子さん，石上美智子さん，草野昌子さん，佐藤亮子さんには，物心両面で大きなご支援をいただきました．以上の方々に深く感謝いたします．墨田郷土資料館，山梨写真館，日野功さんはじめ，多くの方々に，心から御礼申し上げます．

この本の執筆を始めてから，同じ企図を持った2人の友人 — 桜井知佐子さんと鈴木玲之さん — が亡くなりました．天上から応援してくれた知佐子さんと，病床から助言をくださった鈴木さんの励ましが，大きなモチベーションとなりました．本書を戦争で亡くなられたすべての人々，故桜井知佐子さんと故鈴木玲之さんに捧げたいと思います．

References　　参考文献

(1)Association to record the Shizuoka Air Raid (1974) The document of the air raid in Shizuoka city, 464p　静岡空襲を記録する市民の会(1974) 静岡市空襲の記録, 464頁

Shimizu city ed. (1974) The Documents of air raid in Shimizu city, 162p　清水市編(1974) 清水市空襲の記録, 464頁

The Shizuoka Shimbun (1975) Air Raids over Shizuoka prefecture, 277p　静岡新聞社(1975) 大空襲・郷土燃ゆ, 277頁

(2)Association seeking for a Peace (1985) A collection of paintings about Shizuoka Air Raid, 107p　静岡平和を考える市民の会(1985) 画集・街が燃える, 人が燃える, 107頁

Michinori Oki ed. (1994) A Dictionary of Chemistry, Tokyo Kagaku Dojin　大木道則編(1994) 化学辞典, 東京化学同人

Association to promote the Shizuoka Peace Museum (1995) The document of Shizuoka Air Raid, 76p　静岡・平和資料館の設立をすすめる市民の会(1995) ドキュメント静岡の空襲, 76頁

Isao Nakayama (1997) The last air raid for LeMay, Katsura Shobo, 183p　中山伊佐男(1997) ルメイ・最後の空襲, 桂書房, 183頁

Haruo Watanabe (2002) The war on Haruo−The Ship's bombardment on Shimizu wasn't bombing from submarines, Bungeisha, 209p　渡辺晴朗(2002) ハルヲの戦争−清水艦砲射撃, 文芸社, 209頁

Denpachi Izuya cultural Foundation (2002) The architecture of the registered cultural asset – Fukyoraian, 73p　伊豆屋伝八文化振興財団(2002) 登録文化財−不去来庵本堂の建築, 73頁

Japan association for Fire Science and Engineering (2002) The fire and the architecture, Kyoritsu Shuppan, 390p　日本火災学会編(2002) 火災と建築, 共立出版, 390頁

A New edited chart of the Japanese History (2004) Daiichi Gakushusha, 256p　新編日本史図表(2004) 第一学習社, 390頁

(3)Sumida City Museum ed. (2005) Never forget that day, Katsura Shobo, 156p　墨田郷土文化資料館編(2005) あの日を忘れない, 桂書房, 156頁

(4)Association to promote the Shizuoka Peace Museum (2005) The documentary of Shizuoka & Shimizu Air Raids, 132p　静岡平和資料館をつくる会(2005) 静岡・清水空襲の記録, 132頁

(5)Association to promote the Shizuoka Peace Museum (2005) A collection of paintings about Air Raid and Ship's Bombardment on Shizuoka and Shimizu, 109p　静岡平和資料館をつくる会(2005) 静岡清水・大空襲と艦砲射撃, 109頁

Yozo Kudo, Yoshishige Okuzumi (2005) The Atomic Bombing represented by the photographs, 203p　工藤洋三・奥住喜重(2005) 写真が語る原爆投下, 203頁

Yoshishige Okuzumi(2006) The B-29s burned 64 cities, Yoransha,173p　奥住喜重(2006) B-29, 64都市を焼く, 揺籃社, 173頁

Toshio Hikasa, Fumiaki Fujimoto (2007) The 20th AF over Japan, Daigaku Kyoiku Shuppan, 80p　(in Japanese associated with English) 日笠俊男・藤本文昭(2007) 日本上空の米第20航空軍, 大学教育出版, 80頁

Japan Association for Fire Science and Engineering (2007) Principles of Building Fire Safety Engineering, Kyoritsu Shuppan,178p　日本火災学会編(2007) はじめて学ぶ建物と火災, 共立出版, 178頁

Yozo Kudo, Yoshishige Okuzumi (2008) The Air Raid over Japan represented by the photographs, Gendai Shiryo Shuppan, 203p　工藤洋三・奥住喜重(2008) 写真が語る日本空襲, 現代史料出版, 203頁

Yozo Kudo, Nobuhiro Tajima, Yujiro Wada, Hiroko Niitsuma (2009) The effects of the incendiary air raids recorded on the meteorological observatory, Kusyu Tushin No.11, 87p　工藤洋三, 田島伸浩, 和田雄二郎, 新妻博子(2009) 気象観測所の記録に残された焼夷空襲, 空襲通信第11号, 87頁

Hiroko Niitsuma (2009) The temple remained in the Mean Point of Impact in the Shizuoka air raid, Kusyu Tushin No.11, 87p　新妻博子(2009) 爆撃中心点で焼け残ったお堂, 空襲通信第11号, 87頁

Documents of Kambara observation Post (1945)　蒲原防空監視哨資料(1945)

Documents of Fujieda observation Post (1945)　藤枝防空監視哨資料(1945)

Records of the U.S. Strategic Bombing Survey:Tactical Mission Report, No.24, 37, 55, 63, 98, 181, 195, 212, 253, 306, 307 (1945)　米戦略爆撃調査団資料:作戦任務報告書, 第24, 37, 55, 63, 98, 181, 195, 212, 253, 306, 307号(1945)

Records of the U.S. Strategic Bombing Survey:Damage Assessment Reports (1945)　米戦略爆撃調査団資料:損害評価報告書(1945)

Records of the U.S. Strategic Bombing Survey:Air Objective Folders (1942-44)　米戦略爆撃調査団資料:航空目標フォルダー(1942-44)

Records of the U.S. Strategic Bombing Survey:Carrier-Bases Navy and Marine Corps Aircraft Action Report (1945)　米戦略爆撃調査団資料:海軍および海兵隊の艦載機戦闘報告書(1945)

※Materials provided by the Shizuoka Peace Center are as follows : Fig.1~3, 9, 10, 14, 15, 21~23, 25, 27, 30, 34~39, 41~45, 47~49, 52~57　静岡平和資料センター提供資料は以下の通り:図1~3, 9, 10, 14, 15, 21~23, 25, 27, 30, 34~39, 41~45, 47~49, 52~57

カバーイラスト：水野紀子
ページデザイン：杉山友啓

What Happend to People?
Shizuoka Air Raid Documentary
-Real Voices from Japanese Small City-

空から戦争がふってきた
静岡・空襲の記録

2010年6月2日　初版発行

著　者　新妻　博子
発行者　松井　純
発行所　静岡新聞社
　　　　〒422-8033　静岡市駿河区登呂 3-1-1
　　　　TEL：054-284-1666

印刷・製本　株式会社　三創
Ⓒ The Shizuoka Shimbun 2010 Printed in Japan
ISBN978-4-7838-2230-1　C0031

＊定価は表紙に表示してあります。
＊本書の無断複写・転載を禁じます。
＊落丁・乱丁本はお取り替えいたします。